JEFF BUTCHER

WOOD PELLET SMOKER & GRILL COOKBOOK

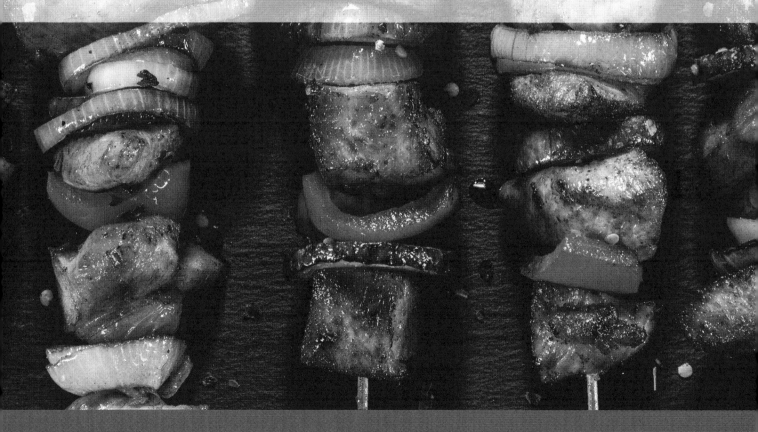

Discover 200 Unique, Tasty, and Authentic Recipes Your
Friends and Family Will Love to Smoke and Grill with
Your Wood Pellet Smoker like a Real Pitmaster

TABLE OF CONTENTS

INTRODUCTION

Cooking food outdoors and sharing it, enjoying it with family and friends can be a pleasure and a real joy. But where to find new ideas and learn about new methods, more varied recipes, and get tastier flavors? This book will help you to achieve that goal! Regardless of your cooking experience level, you'll find all the information you need to get started with wood pellet smokers and grills, extremely useful and fun tools for cooking in a new and easy way. So, if you have tried hard to grill and failed before, you are ready to learn the right way to do it. The results will be mesmerizing and beyond your imagination.

Many people enjoy both grilling foods and smoking foods. Smoking your food on a pellet smoker may be a new concept, but it's an exciting one. With smoking, you can impart additional flavor to your food. Smoking food concentrates the flavors of the ingredients that you are using, such as pepper or maple flavoring. Because smoke is produced using heat, the wood pellets are not burned off completely when the smoking process is completed. This means that flavor is still incorporated into the meat. A wood pellet smoker gives out a nice smokey aroma which lets you add a different flavor to your dish.

To start cooking, you can pick your favorite recipes from the portions of poultry, beef, pork, and seafood. Start by trying recipes from different categories. For instance, try a few recipes on the grill and a few on the smoker. If you would like to give yourself additional options, try smoking the recipe at a higher temperature range. Experimenting with recipes allows you to develop your cooking style and become a master.

When you use a wood pellet smoker in the right way and use the best kind of pellets, the flavor induced is so unique that you will be surprised. You can use smoked meat in just about any recipe that you would typically use meat in. Smoked meat is more succulent, rich in flavor, and more tender than beef cooked conventionally. The flavor characteristics of smoked meat are so diverse that its appeal is hard to resist. All you have to do is bring a little creativity to the smoker's pit, and you can cook anything. When you touch your first piece of smoked meat, you will have realized that you have been missing something in your life. You would have just given birth to yourself. That will be the most memorable day of your life and the best thing that happened to you.

The smoker will help you save money in the long run because you will no longer have to buy meat formerly cooked in it. Smoking might take some time, but the result is worth the wait. Smoked meat can be served either hot or cold. If you have a party planned, you can use the smoker to make a large batch and keep it refrigerated. That way, you will have meat ready for all your guests. The best way to eat smoked meat is to add it to a burger, sandwich, salad, or anything else you come up with. Using the smoker will be your best bet for getting a juicy and tender water-smoking chicken.

Wood pellet smokers and grills are a very low-maintenance way to get a whole lot of cooking done. They require virtually no attention while they are running, the only thing you need to do is dump in pellets every so often, and the food will automatically cook.

They are excellent for people who want to get involved in a brisket or turkey cook but can't be around for a total of 20 hours.

Wood pellet smokers and grills are available in many different sizes, so it's easy to find one that will complement your needs whether you have 2 people or 20.

Many people like these over propane because they are less expensive and can be found almost anywhere. The wood pellets can be purchased at any hardware, home improvement, or building supply store.

You can also find or make your pellet smoker if you want to save money and be able to customize every little thing about the smoker. The most challenging part of making your smoker is building the smoke chamber; everything else is relatively easy.

Enjoy your wood pellet smoker and grill to the fullest. Hope you can share with us some snaps of the dishes you've made with this cookbook. Happy cooking!

1

HOW TO SMOKE?

BASICS OF SMOKING AND GRILLING

Smoke is what you create when a heat source ignites the natural gases inside meat, fish, or vegetables. The US Department of Agriculture defines smoke as "the visible vapor released by the burning of organic substances." Grilling is cooking food over the fire from direct contact with the flame. There are different ways to smoke and grill meats, fish, and vegetables. The charcoal-based methods emit more moisture than electric or gas smokers and produce a smoky flavor while the latter 2 dries out the food being cooked. Choose which method you prefer and the one that best fits your cooking lifestyle.

At its most basic level, smoking and grilling are both methods of cooking food over the fire. There are 5 elements combine to create a good smoker. The heat source is not too strong and not too weak; it's just right. There's enough oxygen in the smoker to keep the wood smoldering consistently without having a devastating impact on temperature. The meat must be placed at an angle so that it gets heat from all sides while allowing smoke to flow around it. The meat must be able to cook slowly, without any flare-ups. It should sit above the smoke layer that rests on top of the chips, wood, or charcoal. There should be a space between the food and the lid to keep flames from burning it or becoming too hot and evaporating all of the juices. This space is called the draft. A constant temperature in a smoker between 250–300ºF is ideal for producing tender meat with a smoky flavor that's not overpowering.

A grill should be about waist high and have enough room for the meat to move when it's flipped. You want a smoker or grill that will allow you to cook food over indirect heat. If you're using a charcoal grill, you'll need to fill the bottom pan with wood chips and leave one side free for placing your meat over the open space. A smoker is designed specifically for cooking foods in a dry environment, so check that your model has vents in the lid to prevent dripping from spoiling your smoky flavor.

DIFFERENCES BETWEEN BARBECUING, OUTDOOR GRILLING, AND SMOKING

Smoke is typically created by burning wood, but it can also be accomplished using different kinds of fuel, such as wood chips, natural gas, or electric heat. There are other terms to describe how the meat is cooked. Barbecue can refer to food that's cooked over direct heat in a very hot environment. Barbecue may also refer to food that's cooked over dry heat, using indirect heat applied high above the food. Barbecue is also used to describe foods that are cooked using the dry heat of the smoke. Barbecuing also refers to cooking foods over indirect heat without using smoke or dry heat. Outdoor grilling uses direct heat in a moderately hot environment and is accomplished using a grill or smoker. A smoker refers to a device that produces smoke, which will often be used in conjunction with flame-cooked food or as part of an outdoor cooking device.

WHAT SMOKER TO CHOOSE?

There are 2 main types of smokers: those that are mechanical and those that are electric. A mechanical smoker is simply a big box with burners or heating elements. The food is placed on racks within the box along with wood chips or chunks and water. When the smoker reaches about 250ºF, flames emerge from the burners, turning the wood into smoke and cooking the meat. One of these smokers can be used to cook both smoked and non-smoked foods, or it can be used as a grill. There's also a second option for a mechanical smoker: the wood pellet smoker. It's a dual fuel-burning device that uses pellets of compressed wood and sawdust or small stones to generate heat in the smoker.

CHOOSING THE BEST WOOD PELLETS FOR YOUR NEEDS

When considering the proper fuel for your smokehouse, you need to have excellent quality pellets. The wood pellet fuel can be purchased online or at tobacco shops, and it offers the same smoking experience as hardwood pellets. Choosing which pellets to use comes down to what type of wood you prefer for smoking and which typically has a long shelf life. For example, hickory does not have a long shelf life, so it's more expensive than apple or cherry wood. Hickory is great for barbecue, but it's so strong that you need to mix it with other wood pellets. Apple or cherry wood is milder than hickory and can be purchased in bulk quantities to reduce the cost per pound. Mesquite has long been known as a smoker's favorite because of its strong flavor and pleasant aroma, which brings out the best in all types of meat.

SELECTING THE RIGHT FOOD AND TEMPERATURE

Smoking different types of meat and fish are not as much about the temperature as it is about moisture. Different meats, such as beef, pork, or chicken, require different types of moisture. Each type of meat needs different amounts of water to keep it moist and juicy while smoking. You can also determine the amount of water needed by looking at the weight of the food you're smoking and dividing that number by 10. The result is the amount of water to add to the wood chips. Choosing a temperature for your smoker is also as simple as picking a higher or lower temperature. The key thing to remember about temperature is that it should not be above 300ºF, as it will damage your meat and making it too chewy. You'll need to monitor the internal temperatures of your meat so that you can adjust the heat accordingly.

When smoking food, you don't want to cook meat at any time other than medium-rare. Cooked meat will have white streaks with purple in the middle; let it cook as much as you want, but no more than that.

WOOD PELLETS AND THE ENVIRONMENT

The big red X on the wood pellet smoker is not a health warning but rather a symbol of the commitment to environmentally friendly smoking. All wood pellet smokers release smoke without burning any fossil fuels, releasing no emissions into the environment. This means that these smokers are carbon-neutral, which helps improve air quality in our communities and may lessen damage to the environment as we know it. The wood pellet smoker is quickly becoming an environmentally friendly way to smoke meat.

TIPS AND TRICKS FOR A GREAT SMOKING AND GRILLING EXPERIENCE

If you're a new smoker, there are a few things that can be done to make the process easier on your first time out. By following these tips, you'll get more smoke, more flavor, and a better smoking experience the first time around.

Don't Fire Up the Smoker Too Early

If you're grilling meat during a meal, wait until it's sizzling on the grill before adding wood chips (unless you enjoy cold food). If you're smoking food ahead of time, wait until 1 hour before you plan to eat before you add wood chips. This way, the smoke will have had enough time to infuse into the meat.

Create Your "Own Recipe" for Smoking

If you don't feel like following a recipe when smoking your food, design your own. There are many variables in smoking meat, and each one can be adjusted to get the flavor you want. Mix and match flavors by adding different types of wood chips to get the taste that you want.

Don't Try to Smoke Meat Without Smoking Wood Chips

If you're looking for a smoky taste, don't use anything other than smoking wood chips. Feel free to mix it up with different types of wood as well. Just make sure they're made for smoking.

When Smoking Meat, Spice It Up

If you want a little kick in the ribs, add some ground red pepper when you add your meat mixture to the smoker. This will add a little flavor and spice to the last few bites of your meat. Do not add salt! Salt will cause the meat to lose moisture and make it tough.

Let It Rest Before Eating

Giving the meat time to rest will ensure that it's at its best when you do eat it. A good resting place for the food is on a cookie sheet set at an angle or on a rack in an empty foil pan. This allows for even airflow around the food and helps with keeping moisture in.

Set Your Meat on Fire

If you want to give it a little extra something, set it on fire. You don't want to do this for the whole time you cook your meat, or you'll end up with burnt and charred bits instead of juicy and flavorful ones.

Learn More About Cooking Techniques

These topping ideas show many other cooking techniques.

2
PORK RECIPES

1. PORK BURNT ENDS

PREPARATION TIME:
15'

COOKING TIME:
4 hours and 15 minutes

SERVINGS:
10

INGREDIENTS:

4 lbs. pork belly
4 tbsps. brown sugar
¼ tsp. cayenne pepper
1 tsp. red pepper flakes
½ tsp. onion powder
½ tsp. garlic powder
1 tbsp. paprika
1 tsp. oregano
1 tbsp. freshly ground black pepper
1 tbsp. salt or to taste
1 tsp. peppermint, dried
1 tbsp. olive oil
¼ cup butter
1 cup BBQ sauce
1 tbsp. maple syrup
2 tbsps. fresh parsley, chopped

DIRECTIONS:

1. Trim pork belly of any excess fat and cut off silver skin. Cut the pork into ½-inch cubes.
2. To make the rub, combine the sugar, cayenne, pepper flakes, onion powder, garlic, paprika, oregano, black pepper, salt, and peppermint in a mixing bowl.
3. Drizzle oil over the pork and season each pork cubes generously with the rub.
4. Preheat your grill to 205°F with the lid closed for 15 minutes.
5. Arrange the pork chunks onto the grill grate and smoke for about 3 hours, or until the pork chunks turn dark red.
6. Meanwhile, combine the BBQ sauce, maple syrup, and butter in an aluminum pan.
7. Remove the pork slices from heat and put them in the pan with the sauce. Stir to combine.
8. Cover the pan tightly with aluminum foil and place it on the grill. Cook for 1 hour or until the internal temperature of the pork reaches 200°F.
9. Remove the pork from heat and let it sit for some minutes.
10. Serve and garnish with fresh chopped parsley.

NUTRITION:

Calories: *477*
Fat: 41.8 g.
Carbohydrates: 19.3 g.
Protein: 6.4 g,

2. BRITISH PORK BELLY

PREPARATION TIME:	COOKING TIME:	SERVINGS:
9'	3 hours and 30 minutes	6

INGREDIENTS:

3 lbs. pork belly, skin removed
Pork and poultry rub as needed
4 tbsps. salt
½ tsp. ground black pepper

DIRECTIONS:

1. Switch on the Smoker grill, fill the grill hopper with apple-flavored wood pellets, power the grill on by using the control panel, select SMOKE on the temperature dial, or set the temperature to 275ºF and let it preheat for a minimum of 15 minutes.
2. Meanwhile, prepare the pork belly and for this, sprinkle pork and poultry rub, salt, and black pepper on all sides of the pork belly until well coated.
3. When the grill has preheated, open the lid, place the pork belly on the grill grate, and shut the grill and smoke for 3 hours and 30 minutes until the internal temperature reaches 200ºF.
4. When done, transfer the pork belly to a cutting board, let it rest for 15 minutes, then cut it into slices and serve.

NUTRITION:

Calories: 430
Fat: 44 g.
Carbs: 1 g.
Protein: 8 g.

3. CHERRY & JALAPEÑO RIBS

PREPARATION TIME:	COOKING TIME:	SERVINGS:
15'	6 hours	4

INGREDIENTS:

1 rack spare ribs
1 (12 oz.) apple's juice
2 jalapeños peppers cut in half, deseeded
3 tbsps. chili powder
2 tbsps. ground cumin
2 tbsps. salt
Black pepper to taste
1 tbsp. garlic, minced
1 tbsp. oregano, dried
1 tsp. celery seeds
1 tsp. dry thyme
½ cup beer
½ cup onion, chopped
¼ cup dry cherries
1 tbsp. BBQ sauce
1 tbsp. olive oil

DIRECTIONS:

1. Get a bowl and mix oregano, salt, cumin, minced garlic black pepper, celery seeds, chili powder, thyme. Mix with a food processor.
2. Put the rib on some aluminum foil and rub the mix all over them.
3. Get the apple juice and add it to the ribs then close the foil into a package. Leave to marinate overnight.
4. Put them on the grill around 5-inch away from the wood pellet (better if Maple).
5. Put the jalapeños on a tray and leave them for 7 minutes under the preheated broiler.
6. Once cooked peel the skin off.
7. Blend them with onion, beer, and cherries. Add some oil and pepper.
8. Put the ribs in the oven at 200ºF for 3–4 hours.
9. Then smoke for 1 hour at 250ºF.
10. Take the foil and the remaining apple juice away and let the ribs cooked in the smoker for 10 minutes or until the surface dries out.
11. Brush with the BBQ sauce and cook for another 15 minutes per side.

NUTRITION:

Calories: 267
Fat: 18 g.
Carbs: 3 g.
Protein: 16 g.

4. TENDER PULLED PORK

PREPARATION TIME:
10'

COOKING TIME:
9 hours

SERVINGS:
12

INGREDIENTS:

9 lbs. pork shoulder, bone-in, fat trimmed
BBQ rub as needed
2 cups apple cider

DIRECTIONS:

1. Switch on the Smoker grill, fill the grill hopper with apple-flavored wood pellets, power the grill on by using the control panel, select SMOKE on the temperature dial, or set the temperature to 250ºF and let it preheat for a minimum of 15 minutes.
2. Meanwhile, prepare the pork shoulder, and for this, season it generously with game rub until well coated.
3. When the grill has preheated, open the lid, place pork should on the grill grate fat-side up, shut the grill, and smoke for 5 hours, and then remove pork from the grill.
4. Take a large baking sheet, line it with 4 large aluminum foil pieces to wrap pork, place pork in the center, bring up the sides of the foil, pour in apple cider, and then wrap tightly.
5. Transfer baking sheet containing wrapped pork on the grill grate and then cook for 4 hours until the internal temperature reaches 204ºF.
6. When done, remove the baking sheet from the grill, let it rest for 45 minutes, then uncover it, place the pork into a large dish and drain excess liquid into a bowl.
7. Shred pork by using 2 forks, remove and discard excess fat and bone, then drizzle with reserved liquid and season with some rub.
8. Serve straight away.

NUTRITION:

Calories: 220
Fat: 15 g.
Carbs: 1 g.
Protein: 20 g.

5. TRADITIONAL PORK STEAK

PREPARATION TIME: 9'	COOKING TIME: 22'	SERVINGS: 4

INGREDIENTS:

2-inch pieces orange peel
2 sprigs thyme
4 tbsps. salt
4 black peppercorns
1 sprig rosemary
2 tbsps. brown sugar
2 bay leaves
10 cups water
4 pork steaks, fat trimmed
BBQ rub as needed

DIRECTIONS:

1. Prepare the brine and for this, take a large container, place all of its ingredients in it and stir until sugar has dissolved.
2. Place all the steaks in it, add some weights to keep the steak submerge into the brine, and let soak overnight.
3. The next day, when ready to cook, switch on the grill, fill the grill hopper with hickory flavored wood pellets, power the grill on by using the control panel, select SMOKE on the temperature dial, or set the temperature to 225ºF and let it preheat for a minimum of 15 minutes.
4. Meanwhile, remove all the steaks from the brine, rinse well, pat dry with paper towels and then season well with game rub until coated.
5. When the grill has preheated, open the lid, place steaks on the grill grate, shut the grill, and smoke for 10 minutes per side until the internal temperature reaches 140ºF.
6. When done, transfer the steaks to a cutting board, let them rest for 10 minutes, then cut into slices and serve.

NUTRITION:

Calories: 250
Fat: 21 g.
Carbs: 1 g.
Protein: 17 g.

6. SWEET WRAPPED SAUSAGES

PREPARATION TIME:
22'

COOKING TIME:
30'

SERVINGS:
6

INGREDIENTS:

12 lbs. bacon strips, halved
14 oz. cocktail sausages
½ cup brown sugar

DIRECTIONS:

1. Place bacon strips in a clean working space, roll them by using a rolling pin, and then wrap a sausage with a bacon strip, securing with a toothpick.
2. Place wrapped sausage in a casserole dish, repeat with the other sausages, place them into the casserole dish in a single layer, cover with sugar and then let them sit for 30 minutes in the refrigerator.
3. When ready to cook, switch on the grill, fill the grill hopper with apple-flavored wood pellets, power the grill on by using the control panel, select SMOKE on the temperature dial, or set the temperature to 350°F and let it preheat for a minimum of 15 minutes.
4. Meanwhile, remove the casserole dish from the refrigerator and then arrange sausage on a cookie sheet lined with parchment paper.
5. When the grill has preheated, open the lid, place cookie sheet on the grill grate, shut the grill, and smoke for 30 minutes. When done, transfer sausages to a dish and then serve.

NUTRITION:

Calories: 270
Fat: 27 g.
Carbs: 18 g.
Protein: 9 g.

7. SWEET AND HOT BBQ RIBS

PREPARATION TIME:
22'

COOKING TIME:
5 h

SERVINGS:
8

INGREDIENTS:

2 racks of pork ribs, bone-in, and membrane removed
6 oz. pork and poultry rub
16 oz. apple juice
8 oz. sweet and heat BBQ sauce

DIRECTIONS:

1. Rub well and marinate for a minimum of 30 minutes.
2. When ready to cook, switch on the Smoker grill, fill the grill hopper with pecan flavored wood pellets, power the grill on by using the control panel, select SMOKE on the temperature dial, or set the temperature to 225°F and let it preheat for a minimum of 15 minutes.
3. When the grill has preheated, open the lid, place pork ribs on the grill grate bone-side down, shut the grill, and smoke for 1 hour, spraying with 10 oz. of apple juice frequently.
4. Then wrap ribs in aluminum foil, pour in the remaining 6 oz. of apple juice, and wrap tightly.
5. Return wrapped ribs onto the grill grate meat-side down, shut the grill, and smoke for 3–4 hours until internal temperature reaches 203°F.
6. Remove wrapped ribs from the grill, uncover them and then brush well with the sauce.
7. Return pork ribs onto the grill grate and then grill for 10 minutes until glazed.
8. When done, transfer ribs to a cutting board, let rest for 10 minutes, then cut it into slices and serve.

NUTRITION:
Calories: 250.8
Fat: 16.3 g.
Carbs: 6.5 g.
Protein: 18.2 g.

8. GRILLED CARNITAS

PREPARATION TIME:
22'

COOKING TIME:
10 h

SERVINGS:
12

INGREDIENTS:

1 tsp. paprika
1 tsp. oregano
1 tsp. cayenne pepper
1 tsp. brown sugar
1 tsp. mint
1 tbsp. onion powder
1 tsp. cumin
1 tsp. chili powder
1 tbsp. salt
1 tsp. garlic powder
1 tsp. Italian seasoning
2 tbsps. olive oil.
2 lbs. pork shoulder roast

DIRECTIONS:

1. Trim the pork of any excess fat.
2. To make the rub, combine the paprika, oregano, cayenne, sugar, mint, onion powder, garlic powder, cumin, chili, salt, and Italian seasoning in a small mixing bowl.
3. Rub all sides of the pork with the rub.
4. Start your grill for smoking, leaving the lid open until the fire starts.
5. Close the lid and preheat the grill to 325°F with the lid closed for 15 minutes.
6. Place the pork in a foil pan and place the pan on the grill. Cook for about 2 hours.
7. After 2 hours, increase the heat to 325°F and smoke pork for an additional 8 hours or until the pork's internal temperature reaches 190°F.
8. Remove pork from it and let it sit until it is cook and easy to handle.
9. Shred the pork with 2 forks.
10. Place a cast-iron skillet on the grill grate and add the olive oil.
11. Add the pork and sear until the pork is brown and crispy.
12. Remove pork from heat and let it rest for a few minutes.
13. Serve.

NUTRITION:

Calories: 514
Fat: 41.1 g.
Carbohydrates: 1.6 g.
Protein: 32 g.

9. STUFFED TENDERLOIN

PREPARATION TIME: 15'	COOKING TIME: 3 h	SERVINGS: 8

INGREDIENTS:

2 pork tenderloin
12 slices bacon
¼ cup Cheddar cheese
¼ cup Mozzarella cheese
1 small onion, finely chopped
1 carrot, finely chopped

For the rub:

½ tsp. garlic, granulated (not garlic powder)
½ tsp. cayenne pepper
1 tsp. paprika
½ tsp. ground pepper
1 tsp. chili
½ tsp. onion powder
¼ tsp. cumin
1 tsp. salt

DIRECTIONS:

1. Butterfly the pork tenderloin and place it between 2 plastic wraps. Pound the tenderloin evenly with a mallet until it is ½-inch thick.
2. Place the cheddar, mozzarella, onion, and carrot on one end of the flat pork. Roll up the pork like a burrito.
3. Combine all the ingredients for the rub in a mixing bowl. Rub the seasoning mixture all over the pork.
4. Wrap the pork with bacon slices.
5. Preheat the grill to 275°F for 10–15 minutes. Use apple, hickory, or mesquite hardwood pellets.
6. Place the pork on the grill and smoke for 3 hours, or until the pork's internal temperature reaches 165°F and the bacon wrap is crispy.
7. Remove the pork from heat and let it rest for about 10 minutes.
8. Cut into sizes and serve.

NUTRITION:

Calories: 241
Fat: 14.8 g.
Carbohydrates: 2.7 g.
Protein: 22.9 g.

10. PORK KEBABS

PREPARATION TIME:
9'

COOKING TIME:
22'

SERVINGS:
4

INGREDIENTS:

2 pork tenderloin, cut into 2-inch cubes
1 large bell pepper, sliced
1 large yellow bell pepper, sliced
1 large green bell pepper, sliced
1 onion, sliced
10 medium cremini mushrooms, destemmed and halved
Wooden or bamboo skewers, soaked in water for 30 minutes, at least

For the marinade:

½ cup olive oil
½ tsp. pepper
1 tsp. salt
1 tbsp. freshly chopped parsley
1 tbsp. brown sugar
1 tsp. Dijon mustard
1 tbsp. soy sauce
1 lemon (juice)
1 tbsp. freshly chopped thyme
1 tsp. minced garlic

DIRECTIONS:

1. In a large mixing bowl, combine all the marinade ingredients. Add the pork and mushroom. Toss to combine. Cover the bowl tightly with aluminum foil and refrigerate for 8 hours.
2. Remove the mushroom and pork from the marinade.
3. Thread the bell peppers, onion, mushroom, and pork onto skewers to make kabobs.
4. Preheat your grill to high with lid closed for 15 minutes, using mesquite hardwood pellets.
5. Arrange the kebobs onto the grill grate and grill for 12 minutes, 6 minutes per side, or until the pork's internal temperature reaches 145°F.
6. Remove kebabs from heat.

NUTRITION:

Calories: 272
Fat: 15.8 g.
Carbohydrates: 9.2 g.
Protein: 24 g.

11. MAPLEWOOD BOURBON BBQ

PREPARATION TIME:	COOKING TIME:	SERVINGS:
15'	2h and 30'	8

INGREDIENTS:

1 large ham
½ cup brown sugar
1 tbsp. bourbon
1 tbsp. lemon juice
2 tbsps. Dijon mustard
¼ cup apple juice
¼ cup maple syrup
1 tsp. salt
1 tsp. freshly ground garlic
1 tsp. ground black pepper

DIRECTIONS:

1. Start your grill on the SMOKE setting, leaving for 5 minutes, until the fire starts.
2. Close the lid and preheat the grill to 325°F.
3. Place the ham on a smoker rack and place the rack on the grill. Smoke for 2 hours or until the internal temperature of the ham reaches 125°F.
4. Combine the sugar, garlic, bourbon, lemon, mustard, apple juice, salt, pepper, and maple syrup in a saucepan over medium to high heat.
5. Bring mixture to a boil, reduce the heat and simmer until the sauce thickens.
6. Glaze the ham with maple mixture.
7. Increase the grill temperature to 375°F and continue cooking until the internal temperature of the ham reaches 140°F.
8. Remove the glazed ham from the grill and let it rest for about 15 minutes.
9. Cut ham into small sizes and serve.

NUTRITION:

Calories: 163
Fat: 4.6 g.
Carbohydrate: 19 g.
Protein: 8.7 g.

12. SOUTHERN GRILLED PORK CHOPS

PREPARATION TIME: 10'	COOKING TIME: 4 h 15'	SERVINGS: 10

INGREDIENTS:

4 pork chops, center-cut, boneless
2 tbsps. olive oil
For the rub:
1 tsp. kosher salt or to taste
1 tsp. Italian seasoning
1 tsp. Greek seasoning
½ tsp. cayenne pepper
1 tsp. brown sugar
1 tsp. finely chopped fresh rosemary
1 tsp. ground black pepper
1 tsp. dried basil
½ tsp. peppermint
½ tsp. oregano
½ tsp. ground cumin

DIRECTIONS:

1. Start your grill on SMOKE mode, leaving the lid open until the fire starts.
2. Preheat grill to 180°F, using hickory hardwood pellets.
3. Combine all the ingredients for the rub ingredients in a small mixing bowl.
4. Drizzle all sides of the pork chops with oil. Liberally season all sides of each pork chop with the rub.
5. Place the pork chops on the grill and smoke, with the lid closed, for 45 minutes.
6. Remove the pork chops from the grill and preheat the grill to 450°F.
7. Return the pork chops to the grill and smoke for 20 minutes or until the pork chops' internal temperature reaches 150°F.
8. Remove the pork chops from the grill and let them rest for about 15 minutes.
9. Slice and serve.

NUTRITION:

Calories: 216
Fat: 12 g.
Carbohydrate: 3 g.
Protein: 25.3 g.

13. PORCHETTA

PREPARATION TIME:
15'

COOKING TIME:
3 h

SERVINGS:
12

INGREDIENTS:

6 lbs. skin-on pork belly
4 lbs. center-cut pork loin
4 tbsps. olive oil
1 cup apple juice
2 garlic cloves, minced
1 onion, diced
1 ¼ cups Pecorino Romano cheese, grated
1 tsp. ground black pepper
1 tsp. kosher salt
3 tbsps. fennel seeds
1 tbsp. freshly rosemary, chopped
1 tbsp. freshly sage, chopped
1 tbsp. freshly thyme, chopped
1 tbsp. lemon zest, grated

For the rub:

1 tbsp. chili powder
2 tsps. grilling seasoning
1 tsp. salt or to taste
½ tsp. cayenne
1 tsp. oregano
1 tsp. paprika
1 tsp. mustard powder

NUTRITION:

Calories: 611
Fat: 23 g.
Carbohydrate: 7 g.
Protein: 90 g.

DIRECTIONS:

1. Butterfly the pork loin and place it in the middle of 2 plastic wraps. On a flat surface, pound the pork evenly until it is ½-inch thick.
2. Combine all the rub ingredients in a small mixing bowl.
3. Place the butterflied pork on a flat surface, cut side up. Season the cut side generously with 1/3 of the rub.
4. Heat 1 tbsp. olive oil in a frying pan over medium to high heat. Add the onion, garlic, and fennel seed. Sauté until the veggies are tender.
5. Stir the apple juice, black pepper, 1 tsp. kosher salt, rosemary, sage, thyme, and lemon zest. Cook for 1 minute and stir in the cheese.
6. Put the sautéed ingredients on the flat pork and spread evenly. Roll up the pork like you are rolling a burrito.
7. Brush the rolled pork loin with 1 tbsp. oil and season with the remaining rub. The loin with butcher's string at the 1-inch interval.
8. Roll the pork belly around the pork, skin side out. Brush the pork belly with the remaining oil and season with 1 tsp. salt.
9. Set a rack into a roasting pan and place the Porchetta on the rack. Pour the wine into the bottom of the roasting pan.
10. Start your grill on smoke mode, leaving the lid open for 5 minutes until the fire starts.
11. Close the lid and preheat the grill to 325°F, using maple or apple hardwood pellets.
12. Place the roasting pan on the grill and roast Porchetta for about 3 hours or until the Porchetta's internal temperature reaches 155°F.
13. Remove the Porchetta from heat and let it rest for a few minutes to cool.
14. Remove the butcher's string. Slice Porchetta into sizes and serve.

'14. PORK JERKY

PREPARATION TIME:
15'

COOKING TIME:
2 h 15'

SERVINGS:
12

INGREDIENTS:

4 lbs. center-cut pork, trimmed of excess fat and sliced into ¼-inch thick slices, boneless

For the marinade:
1/2 cup soy sauce
1 cup Pineapple juice
1 tbsp. rice wine vinegar
1 tsp. black pepper
1 tsp. red pepper flakes
5 tbsps. brown sugar
1 tsp. paprika
1 tsp. onion powder
1 tsp. garlic powder
1 tsp. salt or to taste

DIRECTIONS:

1. Combine and mix all the marinade ingredients in a mixing bowl.
2. Put the sliced pork in a gallon-sized zip-lock bag and pour the marinade into the bag. Massage the marinade into the pork. Seal the bag and refrigerate for 8 hours.
3. Activate the pellet grill smoker setting and leave the lid open for 5 minutes until the fire starts.
4. Close the lid and preheat your pellet grill to 180°F, using a hickory pellet.
5. Remove the pork slices from the marinade and pat them dry with a paper towel.
6. Arrange the pork slices on the grill in a single layer. Smoke the pork for about 2 ½ hours, turning often after the first 1 hour of smoking. The jerky should be dark and dry when it is done.
7. Remove the jerky from the grill and let it sit for about 1 hour to cool.
8. Serve immediately or store in airtight containers and refrigerate for future use.

NUTRITION:
Calories: 260
Fat: 11.4 g.
Carbohydrate: 8.6 g.
Protein: 28.1 g.

15. LEMON PEPPER PORK TENDERLOIN

PREPARATION TIME:	COOKING TIME:	SERVINGS:
22'	23'	6

INGREDIENTS:

2 lbs. pork tenderloin, fat trimmed

For the marinade:

½ tsp. garlic, minced
2 lemons zest
1 tsp. parsley, minced
½ tsp. salt
¼ tsp. ground black pepper
1 tsp. lemon juice
2 tbsps. olive oil

DIRECTIONS:

1. To prepare the marinade, take a small bowl, place all ingredients in it and whisk until combined.
2. Take a large plastic bag, pour marinade in it, add pork tenderloin, seal the bag, turn it upside down to coat the pork, and let it marinate for a minimum of 2 hours in the refrigerator.
3. Fill the grill hopper with apple-flavored wood pellets, power the grill on by using the control panel, select SMOKE on the temperature dial, or set the temperature to 375ºF and let it preheat for a minimum of 15 minutes.
4. When the grill has preheated, open the lid, place pork tenderloin on the grill grate, shut the grill, and smoke for 20 minutes until internal temperature reaches 145ºF, make sure to turn pork halfway.
5. When done, transfer the pork to a cutting board, let it rest for 10 minutes, then cut it into slices and serve.

NUTRITION:

Calories: 289
Fat: 17 g.
Carbs: 6.2 g.
Protein: 26.5 g.

16. CHINESE BBQ PORK

PREPARATION TIME:
9'

COOKING TIME:
2 h

SERVINGS:
8

INGREDIENTS:

2 pork tenderloins, silver skin removed

For the marinade:
½ tsp. minced garlic
½ tbsp. brown sugar
1 tsp. Chinese 5-spice
¼ cup honey
1 tbsp. Asian sesame oil
¼ cup hoisin sauce
2 tsps. red food coloring
1 tbsp. oyster sauce, optional
2 tbsps. soy sauce

For the 5-spice sauce:
¼ tsp. Chinese 5-spice
2 tbsps. brown sugar
1 tsp. yellow mustard
¼ cup ketchup

DIRECTIONS:

1. Prepare the marinade and for this, take a small bowl, place all ingredients in it and whisk until combined.
2. Take a large plastic bag, pour marinade in it, add pork tenderloin, seal the bag, turn it upside down to coat the pork, and let it marinate for a minimum of 8 hours in the refrigerator.
3. Fill the grill hopper with maple-flavored wood pellets, power the grill on by using the control panel, select SMOKE on the temperature dial, or set the temperature to 225ºF and let it preheat for a minimum of 5 minutes.
4. Remove pork from the marinade, transfer marinade into a small saucepan, place it over medium-high heat and cook for 3 minutes, and then set aside until cooled.
5. When the grill has preheated, open the lid, place pork on the grill grate, shut the grill, and smoke for 2 hours, basting with the marinade halfway.
6. Prepare the 5-spice sauce and for this, take a small saucepan, place it over low heat, add all ingredients, stir until well combined and sugar has dissolved and cooked for 5 minutes until hot and thickened, set aside until required.
7. When done, transfer pork to a dish, let rest for 15 minutes, and meanwhile, change the smoking temperature of the grill to 450ºF and let it preheat for a minimum of 10 minutes.
8. Return pork to the grill grate and cook for 3 minutes per side until slightly charred.
9. Transfer pork to a dish, let rest for 5 minutes and then serve with prepared 5-spice sauce.

NUTRITION:
Calories: 281
Fat: 8 g.
Carbs: 13 g.
Protein: 40 g.

17. SMOKED SAUSAGES

PREPARATION TIME:
15'

COOKING TIME:
3 h

SERVINGS:
4

INGREDIENTS:

3 lbs. ground pork
1 tbsp. onion powder
1 tbsp. garlic powder
1 tsp. curing salt
4 tsps. black pepper
½ tbsp. salt
½ tbsp. ground mustard
Hog casings, soaked
½ cup ice water

DIRECTIONS:

1. Fill the grill hopper with flavored wood pellets, power the grill on by using the control panel, select SMOKE on the temperature dial, or set the temperature to 225ºF and let it preheat for a minimum of 15 minutes.
2. Take a medium bowl, place all the ingredients in it except for water and hog casings, and stir until well mixed.
3. Pour in water, stir until incorporated, place the mixture in a sausage stuffer, then stuff the hog casings and tie the link to the desired length.
4. When the grill has preheated, open the lid, and place the sausage links on the grill grate, shut the grill, and smoke for 2–3 hours until the internal temperature reaches 155°F.
5. Transfer sausages to a dish, let them rest for 5 minutes, then slice and serve.

NUTRITION:

Calories: 231
Fat: 22 g.
Carbs: 2 g.
Protein: 15 g.

18. OREGANO PORK TENDERLOIN

PREPARATION TIME:
22'

COOKING TIME:
23'

SERVINGS:
6

INGREDIENTS:

2 lbs. pork tenderloin, fat trimmed

For the marinade:
½ tsp. garlic, minced
1 tbsp. oregano
1 tsp. parsley, minced
½ tsp. salt
¼ tsp. ground black pepper
1 tbsp. soy sauce
2 tbsps. olive oil

DIRECTIONS:

1. Prepare the marinade and for this, take a small bowl, place all of its ingredients in it and whisk until combined.
2. Take a large plastic bag, pour marinade in it, add pork tenderloin, seal the bag, turn it upside down to coat the pork, and let it marinate for a minimum of 2 hours in the refrigerator.
3. When ready to cook, switch on the Traeger grill, fill the grill hopper with apple-flavored wood pellets, power the grill on by using the control panel, select SMOKE on the temperature dial, or set the temperature to 375°F and let it preheat for a minimum of 15 minutes.
4. When the grill has preheated, open the lid, place pork tenderloin on the grill grate, shut the grill, and smoke for 20 minutes until the internal temperature reaches 145°F, turning pork halfway.
5. When done, transfer pork to a cutting board, let it rest for 5 minutes, then cut it into slices and serve.

NUTRITION:
Calories: 267
Fat: 18 g.
Carbs: 3 g.
Protein: 16 g.

19. BACON BBQ BITES

PREPARATION TIME:	COOKING TIME:	SERVINGS:
10'	25'	8

INGREDIENTS:

1 tbsp. fennel, ground
½ cup brown sugar
1 lb. Slab bacon, cut into cubes 1-inch
1 tsp. black pepper
¼ tsp. Salt

DIRECTIONS:

1. Take an aluminum foil and then fold it in half. Once you do that, then turn the edges so that a rim is made. With a fork make small holes on the bottom. In this way, the excess fat will escape and will make the bites crispy.
2. Preheat the grill to 350°F with a closed lid.
3. In a bowl combine the black pepper, salt, fennel, and sugar. Stir.
4. Place the pork in the seasoning mixture. Toss to coat. Transfer on the foil.
5. Place the foil on the grill. Bake for 25 minutes, or until crispy and bubbly.
6. Serve and enjoy!

NUTRITION:

Calories: 300
Fat: 35 g.
Carbs: 5 g.
Protein: 26 g.

20. BACON-WRAPPED SAUSAGES IN BROWN SUGAR

PREPARATION TIME:
20'

COOKING TIME:
30'

SERVINGS:
8

INGREDIENTS:

1 lb. bacon strips, halved
14 oz. cocktail sausages
½ cup brown sugar

DIRECTIONS:

1. Place bacon strips in a clean working space, roll them by using a rolling pin, and then wrap a sausage with a bacon strip, securing with a toothpick.
2. Place wrapped sausage in a casserole dish, repeat with the other sausages, place them into the casserole dish in a single layer, cover with sugar and then let them sit for 30 minutes in the refrigerator.
3. When ready to cook, switch on the grill, fill the grill hopper with apple-flavored wood pellets, power the grill on by using the control panel, select SMOKE on the temperature dial, or set the temperature to 350ºF and let it preheat for a minimum of 15 minutes.
4. Remove the casserole dish from the refrigerator and then arrange sausage on a cookie sheet lined with parchment paper.
5. When the grill has preheated, open the lid, place cookie sheet on the grill grate, shut the grill, and smoke for 30 minutes.
6. When done, transfer sausages to a dish and then serve.

NUTRITION:

Calories: 270
Fat: 27 g.
Carbs: 18 g.
Protein: 9 g.

21. BACON-WRAPPED ASPARAGUS

PREPARATION TIME: 15'	COOKING TIME: 28'	SERVINGS: 6

INGREDIENTS:

15–20 spears (1 lb.) fresh asparagus
extra-virgin olive oil
5 slices bacon, thinly sliced
1 tsp. salt and pepper or your
preferred rub

DIRECTIONS:

1. Break off the ends of the asparagus, then trim it all so they're down to the same length.
2. Separate the asparagus into bundles—3 spears per bundle. Then spritz them with some olive oil.
3. Use a piece of bacon to wrap up each bundle. When you're done, lightly dust the wrapped bundle with some salt and pepper to taste or your preferred rub.
4. Set up your wood pellet smoker grill so that it's ready for indirect cooking.
5. Put some fiberglass mats on your grates. Make sure they're the fiberglass kind. This will keep your asparagus from getting stuck on your grill gates.
6. Preheat your grill to 400°F, with whatever pellets you prefer. You can do this as you prep your asparagus.
7. Grill the wraps for 25–30 minutes, tops. The goal is to get your asparagus looking nice and tender, and the bacon deliciously crispy.

NUTRITION:

Calories: 71
Fat: 3 g.
Carbs: 1 g.
Protein: 6 g.

3
HAM RECIPES

22. CAJUN-HONEY SMOKED HAM

PREPARATION TIME:	COOKING TIME:	SERVINGS:
22'	4 h	15

INGREDIENTS:

1 (5–6 lbs./2.3–2.7 kg.) bone-in smoked ham
1 batch Cajun rub
3 tbsps. honey

NUTRITION:

Calories: 50
Protein: 8 g.
Carbs: 11 g.
Fat: 4 g.

DIRECTIONS:

1. Supply your smoker with wood pellets and follow the manufacturer's specific start-up procedure. Preheat the grill, with the lid closed, to 225ºF (107ºC).
2. Generously season the ham with the rub and place it either in a pan or directly on the grill grate. Smoke it for 1 hour.
3. Drizzle the honey over the ham and continue to smoke it until the ham's internal temperature reaches 145°F (63ºC).
4. Remove the ham from the grill and let it rest for 5–10 minutes, before thinly slicing and serving.

23. ROSEMARY-GARLIC SMOKED HAM

PREPARATION TIME:	COOKING TIME:	SERVINGS:
15'	6 h	12

INGREDIENTS:

1 (10 lbs./4.5 kg.) fresh ham, skinless
2 tbsps. olive oil
1 batch rosemary-garlic lamb seasoning

NUTRITION:

Calories: 111
Protein: 8 g.
Carbs: 15 g.
Fat: 9 g.

DIRECTIONS:

1. Supply your smoker with wood pellets and follow the manufacturer's specific start-up procedure. Preheat the grill, with the lid closed, to 180ºF (82ºC).
2. Rub the ham all over with olive oil and sprinkle it with the seasoning.
3. Place the ham directly on the grill grate and smoke for 3 hours.
4. Increase the grill's temperature to 375°F (191ºC) and continue to smoke the ham until its internal temperature reaches 170ºF (77ºC).
5. Remove the ham from the grill and let it rest for 10 minutes, before carving and serving.

24. BROWN SUGAR-GLAZED HAM

PREPARATION TIME:
31'

COOKING TIME:
5 h

SERVINGS:
15

INGREDIENTS:

1 (12–15 lbs./5.4–6.8 kg.) whole
bone-in ham, fully cooked
¼ cup yellow mustard
1 cup pineapple juice
½ cup light brown sugar, packed
1 tsp. cinnamon, ground
½ tsp. cloves, ground

DIRECTIONS:

1. Supply your smoker with wood pellets and follow the manufacturer's specific start-up procedure. Preheat, with the lid closed, to 275ºF (135ºC).
2. Trim off the excess fat and skin from the ham, leaving a ¼-inch layer of fat. Put the ham in an aluminum foil-lined roasting pan.
3. On your kitchen stovetop, in a medium saucepan over low heat, combine the mustard, pineapple juice, brown sugar, cinnamon, and cloves and simmer for 15 minutes, or until thick and reduced by about half.
4. Baste the ham with half of the pineapple–brown sugar syrup, reserving the rest for basting later in the cook.
5. Place the roasting pan on the grill, close the lid, and smoke for 4 hours.
6. Baste the ham with the remaining pineapple–brown sugar syrup and continue smoking with the lid closed for another hour, or until a meat thermometer inserted in the thickest part of the ham reads 140ºF (60ºC).
7. Remove the ham from the grill, tent with foil, and let rest for 20 minutes before carving.

NUTRITION:

Calories: 107
Protein: 4 g.
Carbs: 9 g.
Fat: 11 g.

25. HAM-WRAPPED SHRIMP WITH PEACH SALSA

PREPARATION TIME:	COOKING TIME:	SERVINGS:
10'	11'	4

INGREDIENTS:

2 lbs. (907 g.) shrimp, peeled and deveined
8 slices prosciutto ham
1 cup water

For the peach salsa:

2 peaches, diced
1 Serrano chili, chopped
2 tbsps. fresh basil, chopped
2 tbsps. honey
2 tbsps. balsamic vinegar
Salt, to taste
Black pepper, to taste

DIRECTIONS:

1. When ready to cook, set the Traeger to HIGH and preheat, lid closed for 15 minutes.
2. In a medium bowl, stir together all the ingredients for the peach salsa.
3. Rinse the shrimp under cold running water and pat dry thoroughly with paper towels. Wrap a piece of prosciutto around each shrimp and secure with a toothpick.
4. Arrange the prosciutto-wrapped shrimp on the grill grate and grill for 4–6 minutes per side, or until the shrimp is opaque.
5. Serve the shrimp warm topped with peach salsa.

NUTRITION:

Calories: 117
Protein: 3 g.
Carbs: 8 g.
Fat: 11 g.

26. BACON CORDON BLEU

PREPARATION TIME:
20'

COOKING TIME:
2 h

SERVINGS:
6

INGREDIENTS:

24 slices bacon
3 large chicken breasts, boneless, skinless, butterfly
3 cups extra-virgin olive oil with roasted garlic flavor
3 Yang original dry lab or poultry seasonings
12 slices black forest ham
12 slices provolone cheese

DIRECTIONS:

1. Weave 4 slices of bacon tightly, leaving extra space on the edges. Bacon weave is used to interlock alternating bacon slices and wrap chicken cordon blue.
2. Slice or rub 2 chicken breast fillets with olive oil on both sides.
3. Sprinkle the seasoning on both sides of the chicken breast.
4. Lay the seasoned chicken fillets on the bacon weave and slice one ham and one provolone cheese on each.
5. Repeat this process with another chicken fillet, ham, and cheese. Fold chicken, ham, and cheese in half.
6. Lay the bacon strips from the opposite corner to completely cover the chicken cordon blue.
7. Use a silicon food-grade cooking band, butcher twine, and toothpick to secure the bacon strip in place.
8. Repeat this process for the remaining chicken breast and ingredients.
9. Using apple or cherry pellets, configure a wood pellet smoker grill for indirect cooking and preheat (180°F–200°F) for smoking. Smoke bacon cordon blue for 1 hour.
10. After smoking for 1 hour, raise the pit temperature to 350°F.
11. Bacon cordon blue occurs when the internal temperature reaches 165°F and the bacon becomes crispy.
12. Rest for 15 minutes under a loose foil tent before serving.

NUTRITION:

Calories: 230
Fat: 2 g.
Carbs: 13 g.
Protein: 38 g.

27. ROASTED WHOLE HAM IN APRICOT SAUCE

PREPARATION TIME:	COOKING TIME:	SERVINGS:
15′	2 h	12

INGREDIENTS:

8 lbs. whole ham, bone-in
16 oz. apricot BBQ sauce
2 tbsps. Dijon mustard
¼ cup horseradish

DIRECTIONS:

1. Fill the grill hopper with apple-flavored wood pellets, power the grill on by using the control panel, select SMOKE on the temperature dial, or set the temperature to 325ºF and let it preheat for a minimum of 15 minutes.
2. Take a large roasting pan, line it with foil, and place ham on it.
3. When the grill has preheated, open the lid, place the roasting pan containing ham on the grill grate, shut the grill, and smoke for 1 hour and 30 minutes.
4. Prepare the glaze and for this, take a medium saucepan, place it over medium heat, add BBQ sauce, mustard, and horseradish, stir until mixed and cook for 5 minutes, set aside until required.
5. After 1 hour and 30 minutes of smoking, brush generously with the prepared glaze and continue smoking for 30 minutes until internal temperature reaches 135ºF.
6. Remove roasting pan from the grill, let rest for 20 minutes, and then cut into slices.
7. Serve ham with remaining glaze.

NUTRITION:

Calories: 157
Fat: 5.6 g.
Carbs: 4.1 g.
Protein: 22.1 g.

4
BEEF RECIPES

28. BLOODY MARY FLANK STEAK

PREPARATION TIME:	COOKING TIME:	SERVINGS:
5'	10-15'	3

INGREDIENTS:

2 cups bloody Mary mix or V8 juice
½ cup vodka
1 whole lemon, juiced
2 garlic cloves, minced
1 tbsp. Worcestershire sauce
1 tsp. ground black pepper
1 tsp. celery salt
½ cup vegetable oil
1 ½ lb. flank steak

DIRECTIONS:

1. Place all ingredients, excluding the flank steak, in a bowl. Mix until well-combined.
2. Put the flank steak in a plastic bag and pour half of the marinade over.
3. Marinate for at least 24 hours in the fridge.
4. When ready to cook, fire your pellet grill to 500°F.
5. Closed the lid and preheat for 15 minutes.
6. Drain the flank steak and pat dry using a paper towel.
7. Place on the grill grate and cook for 7 minutes on each side.
8. Meanwhile, place the remaining marinade (unused) in a saucepan and heat until the sauce thickens.
9. Once the steak is cooked, removed it from the grill, and rest for 5 minutes before slicing.
10. Pour over the sauce.

NUTRITION:

Calories: 719
Protein: 51.9 g.
Carbs: 15.4 g.
Fat: 51 g.

29. PASTRAMI

PREPARATION TIME:	COOKING TIME:	SERVINGS:
10'	4-5 h	12

INGREDIENTS:

1-gallon water, plus ½ cup
1 (3–4 lbs.) pointcut corned beef brisket with brine mix packet
2 tbsps. freshly ground black pepper
¼ cup ground coriander

DIRECTIONS:

1. Cover the beef and refrigerate overnight, changing the water as often as you remember to do so—ideally, every 3 hours while you're awake—to soak out some of the curing salt originally added.
2. Supply your smoker with wood pellets and follow the manufacturer's specific start-up procedure. Preheat with the lid closed to 275°F.
3. Merge the black pepper and ground coriander to form a rub.
4. Drain the meat, pat it dry, and generously coat it on all sides with the rub.
5. Place the corned beef directly on the grill, fat-side up, close the lid, and smoke for 3 hours and 30 minutes.
6. Add the corned beef, cover tightly with aluminum foil, and smoke on the grill with the lid closed for an additional 30 minutes to 1 hour.
7. Remove the meat.
8. Refrigerate.

NUTRITION:

Calories: 123
Fat: 4 g.
Protein: 12 g.

30. SMOKED TEXAS BBQ BRISKET

PREPARATION TIME:	COOKING TIME:	SERVINGS:
30'	**5 h**	**4**

INGREDIENTS:

6 lbs. whole packer brisket
BBQ rub of your choice

DIRECTIONS:

1. Trim the brisket from any membrane and lose fat.
2. Trim the fat side to ¼-inch thick.
3. Season all edges of the brisket with the BBQ rub of your choice and allow resting for 30 minutes inside the fridge.
4. When ready to cook, fire your pellet grill to 275°F.
5. Use mesquite wood pellets when cooking.
6. Close the lid, and then preheat for 15 minutes.
7. Place the brisket fat side up on the grill grate and cook for 5 hours or until the internal temperature reaches 165°F (as read by a meat thermometer).
8. Once cooked, remove the brisket from the grill and allow it to rest before slicing.

NUTRITION:

Calories: 703
Protein: 93.9 g.
Carbs: 0 g.
Fat: 33.4 g.

31. BRAISED MEDITERRANEAN BEEF BRISKET

PREPARATION TIME:	COOKING TIME:	SERVINGS:
30'	5 h	16

INGREDIENTS:

3 tbsps. dried rosemary
2 tbsps. cumin seeds, ground
2 tbsps. coriander, dried
1 tbsp. oregano, dried
2 tsps. cinnamon, ground
½ tsp. salt
8 lbs. beef brisket, sliced into chunks
1 cup beef stock

DIRECTIONS:

1. Mix the rosemary, cumin, coriander, oregano, cinnamon, and salt in a bowl.
2. Massage the spice mix into the beef brisket and allow it to rest in the fridge for 12 hours.
3. When ready to cook, fire your pellet grill to 180°F.
4. Close the lid, and then preheat for 15 minutes.
5. Place the brisket fat side down on the grill grate and cook for 4 hours.
6. After 4 hours, change the heat to 250°F.
7. Continue cooking the beef brisket until the internal temperature reaches 160°F.
8. Remove and place on a foil. Crimp the ends of the foil to make a sleeve.
9. Pour in the beef stock.
10. Return the brisket to the foil sleeve and continue cooking for another hour.

NUTRITION:

Calories: 453
Protein: 33.5 g.
Carbs: 1 g.
Fat: 34 g.

32. GRILLED HAMBURGER WITHOUT FLIPPING

PREPARATION TIME:	COOKING TIME:	SERVINGS:
15'	50'	6

INGREDIENTS:

1 ground beef patties
3 cups Beef rub
6 slices Cheese
6 pcs. Pretzel buns

DIRECTIONS:

1. Start with cold but not frozen patties and sprinkle on the Beef Rub, and massage into both sides of the patty.
2. Preheat grill to 250°F and cook for 45 minutes.
3. Add cheese and other topic varieties of your liking.
4. Close the grill back up and wait for another 10 minutes before removing it.

NUTRITION:

Calories: 696
Fat: 54 g.
Carbohydrates: 11 g.
Protein: 38 g.

33. CHEESEBURGER HAND PIES

PREPARATION TIME:
35'

COOKING TIME:
10'

SERVINGS:
6

INGREDIENTS:

½ lb. lean ground beef
1 tbsp. onion, minced
1 tbsp. steak seasoning
1 cup cheese, shredded
8 slices white American cheese, divided
2 (14 oz.) prepared pizza dough sheets, refrigerated, divided
2 eggs
24 hamburger dill pickle chips
2 tbsps. sesame seeds, for garnish
6 slices tomato, for garnish
Ketchup and mustard, for serving

DIRECTIONS:

1. Supply your smoker thru wood pellets and follow the manufacturer's specific start-up.
2. Preheat with the lid closed to 325°F.
3. On your stovetop, in a medium sauté pan over medium-high heat, cooking the ground beef for 4–5 minutes.
4. Add the minced onion and steak seasoning.
5. Toss in the shredded cheese blend and 2 slices of American cheese and stir until melted and fully incorporated.
6. Remove the cheeseburger mixture from the heat and set it aside.
7. Make sure the dough is well chilled for easier handling.
8. Quickly roll out 1 prepared pizza crust on parchment paper and brush with half of the egg wash.
9. Arrange the remaining 6 slices of American cheese on the dough to outline 6 hand pies.
10. Put the cheeseburger mixture in the 6 pieces of extended dough, top with cheese, and cover with another top of the dough. Tidy the edges with a pizza cutter and press them together with a fork.
11. Bake for 10 minutes. Eat while still warm.

NUTRITION:

Calories: 325
Fat: 21 g.
Carbohydrates: 11 g.
Protein: 23 g.

34. PELLET-GRILLED NEW YORK STRIP

PREPARATION TIME:	COOKING TIME:	SERVINGS:
5'	15'	6

INGREDIENTS:

3 New York strips
Salt and pepper, to taste

NUTRITION:

Calories: 198
Fat: 14 g.
Carbohydrates: 0 g.
Protein: 17 g.

DIRECTIONS:

1. If the steak is in the fridge, remove it 30 minutes before cooking.
2. Preheat the pellet grill to 450°F.
3. Season the steak with salt and pepper.
4. Put it on the grill and let it cook for 5 minutes per side or until the internal temperature reaches 128°F.
5. Rest for 10 minutes.

35. GRILLED BUTTER BASTED PORTERHOUSE STEAK

PREPARATION TIME:	COOKING TIME:	SERVINGS:
5'	8'	4

INGREDIENTS:

4 tbsps. butter, melted
2 tbsps. Worcestershire sauce
2 tbsps. Dijon mustard
Prime rib rub, as needed (you can prepare yours at your liking)
2 porterhouse steaks, 1 ½-inch thick

NUTRITION:

Calories: 515
Protein: 65.3 g.
Carbs: 2.1 g.
Fat: 27.7 g.

DIRECTIONS:

1. Fire the pellet grill and preheat to 255°F. Use desired wood pellets and closes the lid and preheats for 15 minutes.
2. In a bowl, mix the butter, Worcestershire sauce, mustard, and Prime Rib Rub.
3. Massage all over the steak on all sides. Allow steak to rest for 1 hour before cooking.
4. When ready to cook, raise the temperature to 500°F.
5. Put the steaks on the grill grates and cook for 4 minutes on each side or until the internal temperature reads 130°F (as read by a meat temperature) for medium-rare steaks.
6. Take away from the grill and allow resting for 5 minutes before slicing.

36. BRINED SMOKED BRISKET

PREPARATION TIME:
30'

COOKING TIME:
8 h

SERVINGS:
6

INGREDIENTS:

1 cup brown sugar
½ cup salt
1 flat cut brisket
¼ cup beef rub
1 cup water

DIRECTIONS:

1. Make the brine by melting the sugar and salt in 6-quarts of hot water.
2. Allow to cool at room temperature and place the brisket in the solution.
3. Put in the fridge and allow marinating for 12 hours.
4. Remove the brisket from the brine and pat dry with a paper towel.
5. Sprinkle with the beef rub mixture and massage until all surfaces are coated.
6. When ready to cook, fire your pellet grill to 250°F.
7. Close the lid and heat up for 15 minutes.
8. Place the brisket on the grill grate and cook for 4 hours.
9. After 3 hours, double wrap the brisket in foil, turn the temperature to 275°F, and cook for another 3 hours.
10. Unwrap the brisket and grill for 30 minutes more.
11. Detach the brisket from the grill before slicing.

NUTRITION:

Calories: 364
Protein: 48.7 g.
Carbs: 16.6 g.
Fat: 11.6 g.

37. BBQ BRISKET WITH COFFEE RUB

PREPARATION TIME:	COOKING TIME:	SERVINGS:
20'	9 h	10

INGREDIENTS:

5 lbs. whole packer brisket
2 tbsps. coffee rub
1 cup water
2 tbsps. salt

DIRECTIONS:

1. Trim the brisket and remove any membrane.
2. Leave a ¼-inch gap on the bottom.
3. In a bowl, combine the coffee rub, water, and salt until dissolved.
4. Season the brisket with the spice rub and allow to rest in the fridge for 3 hours.
5. When ready to cook, fire your pellet grill to 250°F.
6. Close the lid and heat up for 15 minutes. Move the brisket on the grill grate and close the lid.
7. Cook for 6 hours or up until the brisket's internal temperature reaches 160°F (as read by a meat thermometer).
8. Wrap the brisket in aluminum foil and increase the temperature to 275°F.
9. Cook for another 3 hours.

NUTRITION:

Calories 352
Protein: 47 g.
Carbs: 0 g.
Fat: 16.7 g.

38. PASTRAMI SHORT RIBS

PREPARATION TIME: 30'	COOKING TIME: 3 h	SERVINGS: 4

INGREDIENTS:

2 quarts water
1/3 cup salt
2 tsps. pink salt
¼ cup brown sugar
4 garlic
4 tbsps. coriander seeds
3 tbsps. peppercorns
2 tsps. mustard seeds
2 tbsps. extra-virgin olive oil
1 large ginger ale
2 lbs. beef short ribs

DIRECTIONS:

1. Place all ingredients except for the oil, ginger ale, and short ribs in a large bowl.
2. Mix until well-combined. Add in the short ribs.
3. Marinate the short ribs in the fridge for at least 12 hours.
4. When ready to cook, fire your pellet grill to 300°F.
5. Close the lid and heat up for 15 minutes.
6. Place the short ribs on the grill grate and smoke for 2 hours. Drizzle with oil.
7. Transferred the ribs to a roasting pan and pour enough ginger ale all over the ribs.
8. Cover the pan with foil.
9. Place in the grill and increase the temperature to 350°F and cook for 1 ½ hour.

NUTRITION:

Calories: 521
Protein: 46.7 g.
Carbs: 16.9 g.
Fat: 30.1 g.

39. MEAT CHUCK SHORT RIB

PREPARATION TIME:	COOKING TIME:	SERVINGS:
20'	**5-6 h**	**2**

INGREDIENTS:

4 pcs. bone slab beef chuck short rib, English cut
3–4 cups yellow mustard or extra-virgin olive oil
3–5 tbsps. mustard

DIRECTIONS:

1. Cut the fat cap off the rib bone, leaving ¼-inch fat, and remove the silvery skin.
2. Remove the membrane from the bone and move the spoon handle below the membrane to lift the piece of meat and season the meat properly. Grab the membrane using a paper towel and pull it away from the bone.
3. Apply mustard or olive oil to all sides of the short rib slab. By rubbing it, you can season all sides.
4. Using mesquite or hickory pellets set the wood pellet smoker and grill to indirect heating and preheat to 225°F.
5. Insert a wood pellet smoker and grill or remote meat probe into the thickest part of the rib bone plank. If your grill does not have a meat probe or you do not have a remote meat probe, use an instant reading digital thermometer to read the internal temperature while cooking.
6. Place the short rib bone on the grill with the bone side down and smoke at 225°F for 5 hours.
7. If the ribs have not reached an internal temperature of at least 195°F after 5 hours, increase the pit temperature to 250°F until the meat's internal temperature reaches 195°F–205°F (as read by a meat thermometer).
8. Place the smoked short rib bone under the loose foil tent for 15 minutes before serving.

NUTRITION:

Calories: 357
Carbs: 0 g.
Fat: 22 g.
Protein: 37 g.

40. BALSAMIC VINEGAR MOLASSES STEAK

PREPARATION TIME:
15' + marinating

COOKING TIME:
20-30'

SERVINGS:
4

INGREDIENTS:

1/8 tsp. Pepper
1/8 tsp. Salt
1 tbsp. balsamic vinegar
2 tbsps. molasses
1 tbsp. red wine vinegar
1 cup beef broth
2 ½ lbs. steak of choice

DIRECTIONS:

1. Lay the steaks in a zip-top bag.
2. Add the balsamic vinegar, red wine vinegar, molasses, and beef broth to a bowl. Combine thoroughly by stirring.
3. On the top of the steaks, drizzle this mixture.
4. Place into the refrigerator for 8 hours.
5. Add wood pellets to your smoker and follow your cooker's startup procedure. Preheat your smoker, with your lid closed, until it reaches 350°F.
6. Take the flounced steaks out of the refrigerator 30 minutes before you are ready to grill.
7. Place on the grill, cover, and smoke for 10 minutes per side, or until meat is tender.
8. Place onto plates and let them rest for 10 minutes.

NUTRITION:

Calories: 164
Carbs: 6 g.
Fat: 5 g.
Protein: 22 g.

41. DIJON CORNED BEEF BRISKET

PREPARATION TIME:	COOKING TIME:	SERVINGS:
15'	5 h	5-8

INGREDIENTS:

1 (3 lbs./1.4 kg.) flat cut corned beef brisket, fat cap at least ¼-inch thick
¼ cup Dijon mustard
1 bottle Apricot BBQ Sauce

DIRECTIONS:

1. Remove the brisket from its packaging and discard the spice packet, if any. Soak the brisket in water for at least 8 hours, changing the water every 2 hours.
2. When ready to cook, preheat your pellet grill lid closed for 15 minutes at 300ºF.
3. Place the brisket, fat-side up, directly on the grill, and cook for 2 hours.
4. Pour the remaining ingredients together in a medium bowl. Pour half of the sauce mixture into the bottom of a disposable aluminum foil pan.
5. Using tongs, transfer the brisket, fat-side up, to the pan. Cover the pan tightly with aluminum foil.
6. Return the brisket to the grill and cook for an additional 2–3 hours, or until the brisket is tender and reaches an internal temperature of 203ºF (95ºC), as read by a meat thermometer.
7. Let the brisket cool for 15 minutes. Slice and serve warm.

NUTRITION:

Calories: 385
Carbs: 2 g.
Fat: 30 g.
Protein: 23 g.

42. GEORGE'S SMOKED TRI-TIP

PREPARATION TIME:	COOKING TIME:	SERVINGS:
25'	5 h	4

INGREDIENTS:

1 ½ lb. tri-tip roast
1/8 tsp. Salt
1/8 tsp. Freshly ground black pepper
2 tsps. garlic powder
2 tsps. lemon pepper
½ cup apple juice

DIRECTIONS:

1. Supply your smoker wood pellets and follow the manufacturer's specific start-up procedure. Allow your grill to preheat with the lid closed, to 180°F.
2. Season the tri-tip roast with salt, pepper, garlic powder, and lemon pepper. Using your hands, work on the seasoning into the meat.
3. Place the meat to roast directly on the grill grate and smoke for 4 hours.
4. Pull the tri-tip from the grill and place it on enough aluminum foil to wrap it completely.
5. Increase the grill's temperature to 375°F.
6. Fold in 3 sides of the foil around the roast and add the apple juice. Fold in the last side, completely enclosing the tri-tip and liquid. Return the wrapped tri-tip to the grill and cook for 45 minutes more.
7. Remove the tri-tip roast from the grill and let it rest for 10–15 minutes, before unwrapping, slicing, and serving.

NUTRITION:

Calories: 155
Carbs: 0 g.
Fat: 7 g.
Protein: 23 g.

43. ALMOND CRUSTED BEEF FILLET

PREPARATION TIME:	COOKING TIME:	SERVINGS:
15'	55'	4

INGREDIENTS:

¼ cup almonds, chopped
1 tbsp. Dijon mustard
1 cup chicken broth
1/8 tsp. Salt
1/3 cup onion, chopped
¼ cup olive oil
1/8 tsp. Pepper
2 tbsps. curry powder
3 lbs. beef fillet tenderloin

DIRECTIONS:

1. Rub the pepper and salt into the tenderloin.
2. Place the almonds, mustard, chicken broth, curry, onion, and olive oil into a bowl. Stir well to combine.
3. Take this mixture and rub the tenderloin generously with it.
4. Add wood pellets to your smoker and follow your cooker's startup procedure. Preheat your smoker, with your lid closed, until it reaches 450°F.
5. Lie on the grill, cover, and smoke for 10 minutes on both sides.
6. Continue to cook until it reaches your desired doneness.
7. Take the entire grill and let it rest for at least 10 minutes.

NUTRITION:

Calories: 118
Carbs: 3 g.
Fat: 3 g.
Protein: 20 g.

44. LA ROCHELLE STEAK

PREPARATION TIME:
4 hours and 10 minutes

COOKING TIME:
20'

SERVINGS:
4

INGREDIENTS:

1 tbsp. red currant jelly
½ tsp. salt
½ tsp. pepper
3 tsps. curry powder
8 oz. pineapple chunks in juice
1 ½ lb. flank steak
¼ cup olive oil

DIRECTIONS:

1. Put the flank steak into a large bag.
2. Mix the pepper, salt, red currant jelly, curry powder, pineapple chunks with juice, and olive oil.
3. Pour this mixture over the flank steak.
4. Place into the refrigerator for 4 hours.
5. Add wood pellets to your smoker and follow your cooker's startup procedure. Preheat your smoker, with your lid closed, until it reaches 350°F.
6. Then you are ready to cook the steak, remove the steak from the refrigerator 30 minutes before ready to cook.
7. Lay the steaks on the grill, cover, and smoke for 10 minutes on both sides, or done to your liking.
8. Remove your roasted food from the grill and allow it to cool for about 10 minutes.

NUTRITION:

Calories: 200
Carbs: 0 g.
Fat: 7 g.
Protein: 33 g.

45. BEER HONEY STEAKS

PREPARATION TIME:
10'

COOKING TIME:
20'

SERVINGS:
4

INGREDIENTS:

1/8 tsp. Pepper
1 lemon juice
1 cup beer choice
1 tbsp. honey
1/8 tsp. Salt
2 tbsps. olive oil
1 tsp. thyme
4 steaks your choice

DIRECTIONS:

1. Season the steaks with pepper and salt.
2. Combine with olive oil, lemon juice, honey, thyme, and beer.
3. Rub the steaks with this mixture generously.
4. Add wood pellets to your smoker and follow your cooker's startup procedure. Preheat your smoker, with your lid closed, until it reaches 450°F.
5. Place the steaks onto the grill, cover, and smoke for 10 minutes per side.
6. For about 10 minutes, let it cool after removing it from the grill.

NUTRITION:

Calories: 245
Carbs: 8 g.
Fat: 5 g.
Protein: 40 g.

46. SWEETHEART STEAK

PREPARATION TIME:
5'

COOKING TIME:
15'

SERVINGS:
1

INGREDIENTS:

20 oz. strip steak, boneless, butterflied
2 oz. pure sea salt
2 tsps. black pepper
2 tbsps. raw dark chocolate, finely chopped
½ tbsp. extra-virgin olive oil

DIRECTIONS:

1. On a cutting board, trim the meat into a heart shape using a sharp knife. Set aside.
2. In a lighter bowl, combine the rest of the ingredients to create a spice rub mix.
3. Rub onto the steak and massage until well-seasoned.
4. When ready to cook, fire the pellet grill to 450°F.
5. Closed the lid and preheat for 15 minutes.
6. Grill each side of the steak for 7 minutes.
7. Allow resting for 5 minutes before slicing.

NUTRITION:

Calories: 727
Protein: 132.7 g.
Carbs: 8.8 g.
Fat: 18.5 g.

47. BEEF JERKY

PREPARATION TIME:
6 h 15'

COOKING TIME:
5 h

SERVINGS:
10

INGREDIENTS:

3 lbs. sirloin steaks

For the marinade:
2 cups soy sauce
1 cup pineapple juice
½ cup brown sugar
2 tbsps. sriracha
2 tbsps. hoisin
2 tbsps. red pepper flake
2 tbsps. rice wine vinegar
2 tbsps. onion powder

DIRECTIONS:

1. Mixed the marinade in a Ziploc® bag and add the beef. Mix until well coated and remove as much air as possible.
2. Placed the bag in a fridge and let marinate overnight or for 6 hours. Remove the bag from the fridge 1 hour before cooking.
3. Startup the Wood Pellet Grill and set it on the smoking settings or at 190°F.
4. Lay the meat on the grill leaving a half-inch space between the pieces. Let cool for 5 hours and turn after 2 hours.
5. Remove from the grill and let cool. Serve or refrigerate.

NUTRITION:
Calories: 309
Total fat: 7 g.
Total carbs: 20 g.
Protein: 34 g.

5
LAMB RECIPES

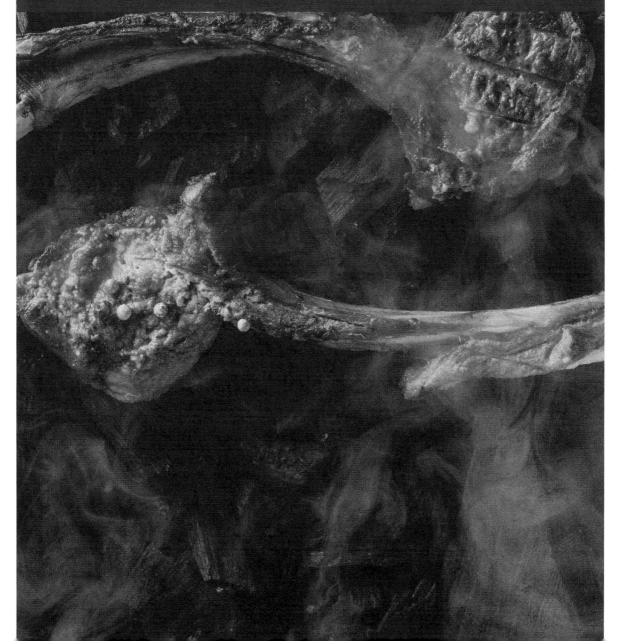

48. LAMB RACK WRAPPED IN APPLE WOOD WALNUT

PREPARATION TIME:	COOKING TIME:	SERVINGS:
25'	60-90'	4

INGREDIENTS:

3 tbsps. Dijon mustard
2 pieces garlic, chopped or 2 cups garlic, crushed
½ tsp. garlic powder
½ tsp. kosher salt
½ tsp. black pepper
½ tsp. rosemary
1 (1 ½ lb.) ram rack, French
1 cup walnut, crushed

DIRECTIONS:

1. Put mustard, garlic, garlic powder, salt, pepper, and rosemary in a small bowl.
2. Spread the seasoning mix evenly on all sides of the lamb and sprinkle with crushed walnuts. Lightly press the walnuts by hand to attach the nuts to the meat.
3. Wrap the walnut-coated lamb rack loosely in plastic wrap and refrigerate overnight to allow the seasoning to penetrate the meat.
4. Remove the walnut-covered lamb rack from the refrigerator and let it rest for 30 minutes to reach room temperature.
5. Set the wood pellet grill for indirect cooking and preheat to 225°F using apple pellets.
6. Lay the grill directly on the rack with the lamb bone down.
7. Smoke at 225°F until the thickest part of the ram rack reaches the desired internal temperature. This is measured with a digital instantaneous thermometer near the time listed on the chart.
8. Place the mutton under a loose foil tent for 5 minutes before eating.

NUTRITION:

Calories: 165
Carbs: 0 g.
Fat: 8 g.
Protein: 20 g.

49. ROASTED LAMB LEG

PREPARATION TIME:
20'

COOKING TIME:
1.5–2 Hours

SERVINGS:
6

INGREDIENTS:

1 leg lamb, boneless
½ cup roasted garlic flavored extra-virgin olive oil
¼ cup parsley, dried
3 garlic, chopped
2 tbsps. fresh lemon juice or 1 tbsp. lemon zest (from 1 medium lemon)
2 tbsps. oregano, dried
1 tbsp. rosemary, dried
½ tsp. black pepper

DIRECTIONS:

1. Remove the net from the lamb's leg. Cut off grease, silver skin, and large pieces of fat.
2. In a small bowl, mix olive oil, parsley, garlic, lemon juice or zest, oregano, rosemary, and pepper.
3. Spice the inside and outside surfaces of the lamb's boneless legs.
4. Secure the boneless lamb leg using a silicone food band or butcher twine. Use a band or twine to form and maintain the basic shape of the lamb.
5. Wrap the lamb loosely in plastic wrap and refrigerate overnight to allow the seasoning to penetrate the meat.
6. Remove the rum from the refrigerator and leave it at room temperature for 1 hour.
7. Set up a wood pellet smoker and grill for indirect cooking and preheat to 400°F using selected pellets.
8. Remove the wrap from the ram.
9. Insert a wood pellet smoker and grill meat probe or remote meat probe into the thickest part of the lamb. If your grill does not have a meat probe or you do not have a remote meat probe, use an instant reading digital thermometer to read the internal temperature while cooking. Roast the lamb at 400°F until the internal temperature of the thickest part reaches the desired finish.
10. Place the lamb under the loose foil tent for 10 minutes, then cut it against the grain and eat.

NUTRITION:
Calories: 200
Carbs: 1 g.
Fat: 13 g.
Protein: 20 g.

50. GREEK LEG OF LAMB

PREPARATION TIME:	COOKING TIME:	SERVINGS:
15'	**25'**	**6**

INGREDIENTS:

2 tbsps. fresh rosemary, finely chopped
1 tbsp. ground thyme
5 garlic cloves, minced
2 tbsps. sea salt
1 tbsp. freshly ground black pepper
1 roll Butcher's string
1 (6–8 lbs.) whole leg lamb, boneless
¼ cup extra-virgin olive oil
1 cup red wine vinegar
½ cup canola oil

DIRECTIONS:

1. In a container, combine the rosemary, thyme, garlic, salt, and pepper; set aside.
2. Using butcher's string, tie the leg of lamb into the shape of a roast. Your butcher should also be happy to truss the leg for you.
3. Rub the lamb generously with olive oil and season with the spice mixture. Put it to a plate, cover it with plastic wrap, and refrigerate for 4 hours.
4. Remove the lamb from the refrigerator but do not rinse.
5. Supply your smoker with wood pellets and follow the manufacturer's specific start-up procedure. Preheat with the lid closed to 325°F.
6. In a small bowl, combine the red wine vinegar and canola oil for basting.
7. Place the lamb directly on the grill, close the lid, and smoke for 20–25 minutes per lb. (depending on the desired doneness), basting with the oil and vinegar mixture every 30 minutes. Lamb is generally served medium-rare to medium, so it will be done when a meat thermometer where inserted in the thickest part reads 140–145°F.
8. Let the lamb meat rest for about 15 minutes before slicing to serve.

NUTRITION:

Calories: 130
Carbs: 2 g.
Fat: 5 g.
Protein: 19 g.

51. SMOKED CHRISTMAS CROWN ROAST OF LAMB

PREPARATION TIME:	COOKING TIME:	SERVINGS:
1 h	2 h	4

INGREDIENTS:

2 racks lamb, trimmed, drenched, and tied into a crown
1 ¼ cups extra-virgin olive oil, divided
2 tbsps. fresh basil, chopped
2 tbsps. fresh rosemary, chopped
2 tbsps. ground sage
2 tbsps. ground thyme
8 garlic cloves, minced
2 tsps. salt
2 tsps. freshly ground black pepper

DIRECTIONS:

1. Set the lamb out on the counter to take the chill off, about 1 hour.
2. In a container, combine 1 cup of olive oil, basil, rosemary, sage, thyme, garlic, salt, and pepper.
3. Baste the entire crown with the herbed olive oil and wrap the exposed drenched bones in aluminum foil.
4. Supply your smoker with wood pellets and follow the manufacturer's specific start-up procedure. Preheat with the lid closed to 275°F.
5. Put the lamb directly on the grill, close the lid, and smoke for 1 hour and 30–2 hours, or wait until a meat thermometer inserted in the thickest part reads 140°F.
6. Remove the lamb from the heat, tent with foil, and let rest for about 15 minutes before serving. The temperature will rise about 5°F during the rest period, for a finished temperature of 145°F.

NUTRITION:

Calories: 206
Carbs: 4 g.
Fat: 9 g.
Protein: 32 g.

52. SUCCULENT LAMB CHOPS

PREPARATION TIME:
15'

COOKING TIME:
20'

SERVINGS:
4

INGREDIENTS:

For the marinade:
½ cup rice wine vinegar
1 tsp. liquid smoke
2 tbsps. extra-virgin olive oil
2 tbsps. onion, dried, minced
1 tbsp. fresh mint, chopped

For the lamb chops:
8 (4 oz.) lamb chops
½ cup hot pepper jelly
1 tbsp. Sriracha
1 tsp. salt
1 tsp. freshly ground black pepper

DIRECTIONS:

1. In a small container, whisk together the rice wine vinegar, liquid smoke, olive oil, minced onion, and mint.
2. Place the lamb chops in an aluminum roasting pan. Pour the marinade over the meat, turning to coat thoroughly. Cover it with a plastic wrapper and marinate it in the refrigerator for 2 hours.
3. Supply your smoker with wood pellets and follow the manufacturer's specific start-up procedure. Preheat, with the lid closed, to 165°F, or the SMOKE setting.
4. Put your saucepan on top of the stove then low heat, combine the hot pepper jelly and Sriracha and keep warm.
5. When you are going to cook the chops, remove them from the marinade and pat dry. Discard the marinade.
6. Season all the chops with salt and pepper, then place them directly on the grill grate, close the lid, and smoke for 5 minutes to "breathe" some smoke into them.
7. Remove the chops from the grill. Increase the pellet cooker temperature to 450°F, or the HIGH setting. Once your griller is up to temperature, place the chops on the grill and sear, cooking for 2 minutes per side to achieve medium-rare chops. A meat thermometer that is usually inserted in the thickest part of the meat should read 145°F. Continue grilling, if necessary, to your desired doneness.
8. Serve the chops with the warm Sriracha pepper jelly on the side.

NUTRITION:
Calories: 277
Carbs: 0 g.
Fat: 26 g.
Protein: 18 g.

53. ROASTED ROSEMARY LAMB

PREPARATION TIME:
15'

COOKING TIME:
4 h

SERVINGS:
2

INGREDIENTS:

1 lamb rack
2 rosemary sprigs, chopped
Salt and pepper to taste
12 baby potatoes
½ cup butter
1 bunch asparagus
2 tbsps. olive oil

DIRECTIONS:

1. Set your wood pellet grill to 225°F. Sprinkle the lamb with rosemary, salt, and pepper.
2. In a baking pan, add the potatoes and coat with the butter. Add the lamb to the grill.
3. Place the pan with potatoes beside the lamb. Roast for 3 hours.
4. Coat the asparagus with olive oil. In your last 20 minutes of cooking, stir the asparagus into the potatoes.
5. Serve the lamb with asparagus and baby potatoes.

NUTRITION:

Calories: 197
Carbs: 3 g.
Fat: 14 g.
Protein: 15 g.

54. GRILLED LAMB

PREPARATION TIME:
10'

COOKING TIME:
1 h

SERVINGS:
6

INGREDIENTS:

2 racks lamb, fat trimmed
2 tbsps. Dijon mustard
2 cups Steak seasoning
1 tsp. fresh rosemary, chopped
1 tbsp. fresh parsley, chopped

NUTRITION:

Calories: 241   Fat: 17 g.
Carbs: 0 g.   Protein: 21 g.

DIRECTIONS:

1. Coat the lamb with the mustard.
2. Sprinkle all sides with seasoning, rosemary, and parsley.
3. Set your wood pellet grill to 400ºF.
4. Sear the meat side of the lamb for 6 minutes.
5. Reduce temperature to 300ºF.
6. Grill it for about 20 minutes, turning once or twice.
7. Let rest for 10 minutes before slicing and serving.

55. CHIPOTLE LAMB

PREPARATION TIME:
15'

COOKING TIME:
2 h 30'

SERVINGS:
6

INGREDIENTS:

1 rack lamb ribs
¾ cup olive oil
Pepper to taste
1 tbsp. chipotle powder
3 garlic cloves
¼ cup applewood bacon rub
2 tbsps. rosemary, chopped
2 tbsps. thyme, chopped
2 tbsps. sage, chopped
2 tbsps. parsley

DIRECTIONS:

1. Coat the lamb ribs with olive oil. Season with pepper and chipotle powder.
2. Marinate for 15 minutes. Set your wood pellet grill to 275ºF.
3. Combine the rest of the ingredients. Spread the mixture on all sides of the lamb.
4. Cook the lamb for 2 hours. Allow it to rest about 10 minutes before carving and serving.

NUTRITION:

Calories: 210   Fat: 13 g.
Carbs: 0 g.   Protein: 22 g.

56. HICKORY RACK OF LAMB

PREPARATION TIME:
10'

COOKING TIME:
2 h

SERVINGS:
3

INGREDIENTS:

1 (3 lbs.) rack lamb, drenched

For the marinade:
1 lemon juice
1 tsp. ground black pepper
1 tsp. thyme
¼ cup balsamic vinegar
1 tsp. basil, dried
2 tbsps. Dijon mustard
2 garlic cloves, crushed

For the rub:
½ tsp. cayenne pepper
½ tsp. ground black pepper
¼ tsp. Italian seasoning
1 tsp. oregano
1 tsp. mint, dried
1 tsp. paprika
1 tsp. garlic powder
1 tsp. onion powder
1 tsp. parsley, dried
1 tsp. basil, dried
1 tsp. rosemary, dried
4 tbsps. olive oil

DIRECTIONS:

1. Put all the marinade ingredients in an empty container. Pour the marinade into a gallon zip-lock bag. Add the rack of lamb and massage the marinade into the rack. Seal the bag and place it in a refrigerator. Refrigerate for 8 hours or overnight.
2. When ready to roast, remove the rack of lamb from the marinade and let it sit for about 2 hours or until it is at room temperature.
3. Meanwhile, combine all the rub ingredients except the olive oil in a mixing bowl.
4. Rub the rub mixture over the rack of lamb generously. Drizzle rack with olive oil.
5. Start your grill on smoke with the lid open until the fire starts.
6. Close the lid and preheat the grill to 225°F using hickory wood pellets.
7. Place the rack of your lamb on the grill grate, bone side down. Smoke it for about 2 hours or until the internal temperature of the meat reaches 140–145°F.
8. Take off the rack of lamb from the grill and let it rest for about 10 minutes to cool.

NUTRITION:
Calories: 800
Fat: 41.1 g.
Carbs: 6.7 g.
Protein: 93.8 g.

57. LEG OF LAMB

PREPARATION TIME:
10'

COOKING TIME:
2 h

SERVINGS:
6

INGREDIENTS:

1 (2 lbs.) leg lamb
1 tsp. rosemary, dried
2 tsps. freshly ground black pepper
4 garlic cloves, minced
2 tsps. salt or more to taste
½ tsp. paprika
1 tsp. thyme
2 tbsps. olive oil
1 tsp. brown sugar
2 tbsps. oregano

DIRECTIONS:

1. Trim the meat of excess fat and remove silver skin.
2. In a mixing bowl, combine the thyme, rosemary, salt, sugar, oregano, paprika, black pepper, garlic, and olive oil.
3. Generously, rub the mixture over the leg of lamb. Cover seasoned leg of lamb with foil and let it sit for 1 hour to marinate.
4. Start your grill on SMOKE and leave the lid open for 5 minutes, or until the fire starts. Cover the lid and preheat the grill to 250°F using hickory, maple, or applewood pellets.
5. Remove the foil and place the leg of lamb on a smoker rack. Place the rack on the grill and smoke the leg of lamb for about 4 hours or until it reaches the internal temperature of your meat 145°F. Take off the leg of lamb from the grill and let it rest for a few minutes to cool. Cut into sizes and serve.

NUTRITION:

Calories: 334
Fat: 16 g.
Carbs: 2.9 g.
Protein: 42.9 g.

58. SMOKED LAMB CHOPS

PREPARATION TIME:
10'

COOKING TIME:
50'

SERVINGS:
4

INGREDIENTS:

1 rack lamb, fat trimmed
2 tbsps. fresh rosemary
2 tbsps. sage, fresh
1 tbsp. garlic cloves, roughly
chopped
½ tbsp. salt
½ tbsp. pepper, coarsely ground
¼ cup olive oil
1 tbsp. honey

DIRECTIONS:

1. Preheat your wood pellet smoker to 225°F using fruitwood. Put all your ingredients except the lamb in a food processor. Liberally apply the mixture to the lamb.
2. Place the lamb on the smoker for 45 minutes or until the internal temperature reaches 120°F.
3. Sear the lamb on the grill for 2 minutes per side. Let rest for 5 minutes before serving. Slice and enjoy.

NUTRITION:

Calories: 704
Fat: 56 g.
Carbs: 24 g.
Protein: 27 g.

59. WOOD-PELLET-SMOKED LAMB SHOULDER

PREPARATION TIME: 10'	COOKING TIME: 1 h 30'	SERVINGS: 7

INGREDIENTS:

For the smoked lamb shoulder:

5 lbs. lamb shoulder, boneless and excess fat trimmed
2 tbsps. kosher salt
2 tbsps. black pepper
1 tbsp. rosemary, dried
1 cup water
1 tbsp. oil

For the injection:

1 cup apple cider vinegar

For the spritz:

1 cup apple cider vinegar
1 cup apple juice

DIRECTIONS:

1. Preheat the wood pellet smoker with a water pan to 225°F.
2. Rinse the lamb in cold water then pat it dry with a paper towel. Inject vinegar into the lamb.
3. Pat the lamb dry again and rub with oil, salt black pepper, and rosemary. Tie with kitchen twine.
4. Smoke uncovered for 1 hour then spritz after every 15 minutes until the internal temperature reaches 195°F.
5. Take off the lamb from the grill and place it on a platter. Let cool before shredding it and enjoying it with your favorite side.

NUTRITION:

Calories: 243
Fat: 19 g.
Carbs: 0 g.
Protein: 17 g.

60. WOOD-PELLET-SMOKED PULLED LAMB SLIDERS

PREPARATION TIME:	COOKING TIME:	SERVINGS:
10'	7 h	7

INGREDIENTS:

For the lamb's shoulder
5 lbs. lamb shoulder, boneless
½ cup olive oil
¼ cup dry rub
10 oz. spritz

For the dry rub:
1/3 cup kosher salt
1/3 cup pepper, ground
1/3 cup garlic, granulated

For the spritz:
4 oz. Worcestershire sauce
6 oz. apple cider vinegar

DIRECTIONS:

1. Preheat the wood pellet smoker with a water bath to 250ºF.
2. Trim any fat from the lamb then rub with oil and dry rub.
3. Place the lamb on the smoker for 90 minutes then spritz with a spray bottle every 30 minutes until the internal temperature reaches 165ºF.
4. Transfer the lamb shoulder to a foil pan with the remaining spritz liquid and cover tightly with foil.
5. Place back in the smoker and smoke until the internal temperature reaches 200ºF.
6. Remove from the smoker and let rest for 30 minutes before pulling the lamb and serving with slaw, bun, or aioli. Enjoy

NUTRITION:
Calories: 339
Fat: 22 g.
Carbs: 16 g.
Protein: 18 g.

61. SMOKED LAMB MEATBALLS

PREPARATION TIME:
10'

COOKING TIME:
1 h

SERVINGS:
5

INGREDIENTS:

1 lb. lamb shoulder, ground
3 garlic cloves, finely diced
3 tbsps. shallot, diced
1 tbsp. salt
1 egg
½ tbsp. pepper
½ tbsp. cumin
½ tbsp. smoked paprika
¼ tbsp. red pepper flakes
¼ tbsp. cinnamon, ground
¼ cup panko breadcrumbs

DIRECTIONS:

1. Set the wood pellet smoker to 250ºF using fruitwood.
2. In a mixing bowl, combine all meatball ingredients until well mixed.
3. Form small-sized balls and place them on a baking sheet. Place the baking sheet in the smoker and smoke until the internal temperature reaches 160ºF.
4. Remove from the smoker and serve. Enjoy.

NUTRITION:

Calories: 73
Fat: 5.2 g.
Carbs: 1.5 g.
Protein: 4.9 g.

62. CROWN RACK OF LAMB

PREPARATION TIME:
10'

COOKING TIME:
30'

SERVINGS:
6

INGREDIENTS:

2 racks lamb, drenched
1 tbsp. garlic, crushed
1 tbsp. rosemary, finely chopped
¼ cup olive oil
2 feet twine

DIRECTIONS:

1. Rinse the racks with cold water then pat them dry with a paper towel.
2. Lay the racks on a flat board then score between each bone, about ¼-inch down.
3. In a mixing bowl, mix garlic, rosemary, and oil then generously brush on the lamb.
4. Take each lamb rack and bend it into a semicircle forming a crown-like shape.
5. Use the twine to wrap the racks about 4 times starting from the base to the top. Make sure you tie the twine tightly to keep the racks together.
6. Preheat the wood pellet to 400-450ºF then place the lamb racks on a baking dish. Place the baking dish on the pellet grill.
7. Cook for 10 minutes then reduces the temperature to 300ºF. Cook for 20 more minutes or until the internal temperature reaches 130ºF.
8. Remove the lamb rack from the wood pellet and let rest for 15 minutes.
9. Serve when hot with veggies and potatoes. Enjoy.

NUTRITION:

Calories: 390
Fat: 35 g.
Carbs: 0 g.
Protein: 17 g.

63. WOOD-PELLET-SMOKED LEG OF LAMB

PREPARATION TIME:
15'

COOKING TIME:
3 h

SERVINGS:
6

INGREDIENTS:

1 leg lamb, boneless
4 garlic cloves, minced
2 tbsps. salt
1 tbsp. black pepper, freshly ground
2 tbsps. oregano
1 tbsp. thyme
2 tbsps. olive oil

DIRECTIONS:

1. Cut off any excess fat from the lamb and tie the lamb using twine to form a nice roast.
2. In a mixing bowl, minced garlic, spices, and oil. Rub all over the lamb, wrap with a plastic bag then refrigerate for 1 hour to marinate.
3. Place the lamb on a smoker set at 250ºF. Smoke the lamb for 4 hours or until the internal temperature reaches 145ºF.
4. Remove from the smoker and let it rest to cool. Serve and enjoy.

NUTRITION:

Calories 356
Fat 16 g.
Carbs 3 g.
Protein 49 g.

64. WOOD-PELLET-GRILLED AUSSIE LEG OF LAMB ROAST

PREPARATION TIME:	COOKING TIME:	SERVINGS:
30'	2 h	8

INGREDIENTS:

5 lbs. Aussie leg of lamb, boneless

For the smoked paprika rub:
1 tbsp. raw sugar
1 tbsp. kosher salt
1 tbsp. black pepper
1 tbsp. smoked paprika
1 tbsp. garlic powder
1 tbsp. rosemary, dried
1 tbsp. onion powder
1 tbsp. cumin
½ tbsp. cayenne pepper

For the roasted carrots:
1 bunch rainbow carrots
1 tbsp. Olive oil
1/8 tsp. Salt
1/8 tsp. Pepper

DIRECTIONS:

1. Heat the wood pellet grill to 375ºF.
2. Trim any excess fat from the lamb.
3. Put all your rub ingredients and rub all over the lamb. Place the lamb on the grill and smoke for 2 hours.
4. Toss the carrots in oil, salt, and pepper then add to the grill after the lamb has cooked for 1 ½ hour.
5. Cook until the roast internal temperature reaches 135ºF. remove the lamb from the grill and cover with foil. Let rest for 30 minutes.
6. Remove the carrots from the grill once soft and serve with the lamb. Enjoy.

NUTRITION:
Calories: 257
Fat: 8 g.
Carbs: 6 g.
Protein: 37 g.

65. SIMPLE-GRILLED LAMB CHOPS

PREPARATION TIME: 10'	COOKING TIME: 6'	SERVINGS: 6

INGREDIENTS:

¼ cup distilled white vinegar
2 tbsps. salt
½ tbsp. black pepper
1 tbsp. garlic, minced
1 onion, thinly sliced
2 tbsps. olive oil
2 lbs. lamb chops

DIRECTIONS:

1. In a resealable bag, mix vinegar, salt, black pepper, garlic, sliced onion, and oil until all salt has dissolved.
2. Add the lamb chops and toss until well coated. Place in the fridge to marinate for 2 hours.
3. Preheat the wood pellet grill to high heat.
4. Remove the lamb from the fridge and discard the marinade. Wrap any exposed bones with foil.
5. Grill your lamb meat for 3 minutes per side. You can also broil in a broiler for more crispness. Serve and enjoy

NUTRITION:

Calories: 519
Fat: 44.8 g.
Carbs: 2.3 g.
Protein: 25 g.

66. WOOD-PELLET-GRILLED LAMB WITH BROWN SUGAR GLAZE

PREPARATION TIME:	COOKING TIME:	SERVINGS:
15'	10'	4

INGREDIENTS:

¼ cup brown sugar
2 tbsps. ginger, ground
2 tbsps. tarragon, dried
1 tsp. cinnamon, ground
1 tbsp. ground black pepper
1 tbsp. garlic powder
½ tbsp. salt
4 lamb chops

DIRECTIONS:

1. In a mixing bowl, mix sugar, ginger, dried tarragon, cinnamon, black pepper, garlic powder, and salt.
2. Rub the lamb chops with the seasoning and place them on a plate. Refrigerate for an hour to marinate.
3. Preheat the grill to high heat then brush the grill grate with oil.
4. Arrange the lamb chops on the grill grate in a single layer and cook for 5 minutes on each side. Serve and enjoy.

NUTRITION:

Calories: 241
Fat 13.1 g.
Carbs: 15.8 g.
Protein: 14.6 g.

67. GRILLED LEG OF LAMBS STEAKS

PREPARATION TIME:
10'

COOKING TIME:
10'

SERVINGS:
4

INGREDIENTS:

4 lamb steaks, bone-in
¼ cup olive oil
4 garlic cloves, minced
1 tbsp. rosemary, freshly chopped
Salt and black pepper to taste

DIRECTIONS:

1. Put the lamb in a shallow container in a single layer. Top with oil, garlic cloves, rosemary, salt, and black pepper then flip the steaks to cover on both sides.
2. Let sit for 30 minutes to marinate.
3. Preheat the wood pellet grill to high and brush the grill grate with oil.
4. Place the lamb steaks on the grill grate and cook until browned and the internals are slightly pink. The internal temperature should be 140°F.
5. Let rest for 5 minutes before serving. Enjoy.

NUTRITION:

Calories: 327
Fat: 21.9 g.
Carbs: 1.7 g.
Protein: 29.6 g.

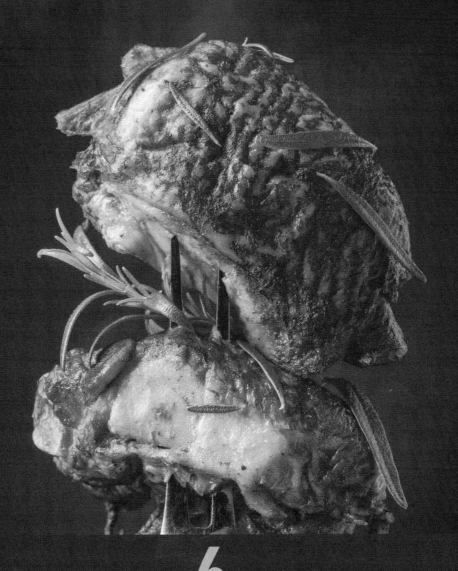

6

CHICKEN RECIPES

68. TERIYAKI CHICKEN WINGS WITH SESAME DRESSING

PREPARATION TIME:
20'

COOKING TIME:
1 h 10'

SERVINGS:
6

INGREDIENTS:

1kg. Chicken wings

For the teriyaki glaze:
2/3 cup mirin
2 tbsps. ginger, minced
3 tbsps. cornstarch
2 tbsps. rice vinegar
1 cup soy sauce
1/3 cup brown sugar
8 garlic cloves, minced
2 tsps. sesame oil
3 tbsps. water

For the creamy sesame dressing:
1 green onion, chopped
½ cup mayonnaise
¼ cup rice wine vinegar
1 tsp. garlic, ground
1 tbsp. soy sauce
2 tbsps. sesame oil
½ tsp. ginger, ground
1 tsp. sriracha
2 tbsps. maple syrup
Salt and pepper to taste

NUTRITION:
Calories: 256
Fat: 5 g.
Carbs: 27 g.
Protein: 29 g.

DIRECTIONS:

1. Use the light pellets for the sake of getting the smoky flavor.
2. Set the grill to the SMOKE mode by keeping the temperature to 225ºF.
3. Now trim the wings and make them into drumettes and season with sea salt and black pepper.
4. Smoke them for nearly 45 minutes.

For the teriyaki glaze:
5. Mince both garlic and ginger by using a tsp. of sesame oil.
6. Then mix all the ingredients except for cornstarch and water.
7. Take a pan and boil cornstarch and water on low heat.
8. Simmer for 15 minutes and then, when done, mix it with an immersion blender.
9. Add cornstarch and water and stir it until it has mixed well.
10. Add this mix to the teriyaki glaze and mix it well until it thickens. Set it aside.

For the creamy dressing:
11. Take a blender and blend all the ingredients thoroughly until you get a smooth mixture.
12. Set the grill for direct flame grilling and put the temperature to medium.
13. Grill the wings for approximately 10 minutes.
14. The internal temperature should reach 165ºF when you remove the wings from the grill.
15. Toss them in the glaze when done.
16. Sprinkle some sesame seeds along with the green onion.
17. Serve hot and spicy.

69. SPICED LEMON CHICKEN

PREPARATION TIME:
20'

COOKING TIME:
1 h 10'

SERVINGS:
1

INGREDIENTS:

1 whole chicken
4 garlic cloves, minced
2 lemons zest
1 tbsp. olive oil
1 tbsp. smoked paprika
1 ½ tsp. salt
½ tsp. black pepper
½ tsp. oregano, dried
1 tbsp. ground cumin

DIRECTIONS:

1. Preheat the grill by pushing the temperature to 375ºF.
2. Take the chicken and spatchcock it by cutting it on both sides right from the backbone to the tail via the neck.
3. Lay it flat and push it down on the breastbone. This would break the ribs.
4. Take all the leftover ingredients in a bowl except ½ tsp. of salt and crush them to make a smooth rub.
5. Spread this rub evenly over the chicken, making sure that it seeps right under the skin.
6. Place the chicken on the grill grates and cook for 1 hour until the internal temperature reads 165ºF. Let it rest for 10 minutes.
7. Serve and enjoy.

NUTRITION:

Calories: 178
Fat: 9 g.
Protein: 23 g.

70. SLOW ROASTED SHAWARMA

PREPARATION TIME:	COOKING TIME:	SERVINGS:
20'	4 h 10'	1

INGREDIENTS:

5 ½ lbs. chicken thighs, boneless, skinless
4 ½ lbs. lamb fat
Pita bread
5 ½ lbs. top sirloin
2 large yellow onions
4 tbsps. rub
Desired toppings like pickles, tomatoes, fries, salad, and more

DIRECTIONS:

1. Slice the meat and fat into ½-inch slices and place them in 3 separate bowls.
2. Season each of the bowls with the rub and massage them into the meat to make sure it seeps well.
3. Place half of the onion at the base of each half skewer.
4. Add 2 layers from each of the bowls at a time.
5. Put the other 2 half onions at the top, wrap them in plastic and let it refrigerate overnight.
6. Set the grill to preheat, keeping the temperature to 275ºF.
7. Lay the Shawarma on the grill grate and let it cook for approximately 4 hours. Make sure to turn it in at least once.
8. Remove from the grill and shoot the temperature to 445ºF. Place a cast iron griddle on the grill grate and pour it with olive oil.
9. When the griddle has turned hot, place the whole shawarma on the cast iron and smoke it for 5–10 minutes per side.
10. Remove from the grill and slice off the edges. Repeat the same with the leftover shawarma.
11. Serve in pita bread and add the chosen toppings.

NUTRITION:

Calories: 585
Fat: 40 g.
Carbs: 9 g.
Protein: 46 g.

71. BAKED GARLIC PARMESAN WINGS

PREPARATION TIME: 20'

COOKING TIME: 30'

SERVINGS: 1

INGREDIENTS:

5 lbs. chicken wings
½ cup chicken rub

For the garnish:

1 cup Parmesan cheese, shredded
3 tbsps. parsley, chopped

For the sauce:

10 garlic cloves, finely diced
1 cup butter
2 tbsps. chicken rub

DIRECTIONS:

1. Set the grill on preheat by keeping the temperature high.
2. Take a large bowl and toss the wings in it along with the chicken rub.
3. Place the wings directly on the grill grate and cook it for 10 minutes.
4. Flip it and cook for the next 10 minutes.
5. Check the internal temperature, and it needs to reach in the range of 165–180ºF.
6. To make the garlic sauce, take a midsized saucepan and mix garlic, butter, and the leftover rub.
7. Cook it over medium heat on a stovetop for 10 minutes while stirring in between to avoid the making of lumps.
8. When the wings have been cooked, remove them from the grill and place them in a large bowl.
9. Toss the wings with garlic sauce along with parsley and Parmesan cheese.
10. Serve and enjoy.

NUTRITION:

Calories: 90
Fat: 8 g.
Carbs: 1 g.
Protein: 4 g.

72. CAJUN PATCH COCK CHICKEN

PREPARATION TIME:	COOKING TIME:	SERVINGS:
30'	2 h 30'	4

INGREDIENTS:

4–5 lbs. fresh or thawed frozen chicken

4–6 glasses extra-virgin olive oil

4 tbsps. Cajun Spice or Lucille's® Bloody Mary Mix Cajun Hot Dry Herb Mix Seasoning

DIRECTIONS:

1. Place the chicken breast on a cutting board with the chest down.
2. Using kitchen or poultry scissors, cut along the side of the spine and remove.
3. Turn the chicken over and press down firmly on the chest to flatten it. Carefully loosen and remove the skin on the chest, thighs, and drumsticks.
4. Rub olive oil freely under and on the skin. Season chicken in all directions and apply directly to the meat under the skin.
5. Wrap the chicken in plastic wrap and place it in the refrigerator for 3 hours to absorb the flavor.
6. Use hickory, pecan pellets, or blend to configure a wood pellet smoker grill for indirect cooking and preheat to 225°F.
7. If the unit has a temperature meat probe input, such as a MAK Grills 2 Star, insert the probe into the thickest part of the breast. Make chicken for 1 ½ hour.
8. After 1 ½ hour at 225°F, raise the pit temperature to 375°F and roast until the inside temperature of the thickest part of the chest reaches 170°F and the thighs are at least 180°F.
9. Place the chicken under a loose foil tent for 15 minutes before carving.

NUTRITION:

Calories: 308
Fat: 18 g.
Carbs: 1 g.
Protein: 30 g.

73. ROASTED TUSCAN THIGHS

PREPARATION TIME:
20'

COOKING TIME:
40-60'

SERVINGS:
6

INGREDIENTS:

8 chicken thighs, with bone, with skin
3 extra-virgin olive oils with roasted garlic flavor
3 cups Tuscan or Tuscan seasoning per thigh

DIRECTIONS:

1. Cut off excess skin-on chicken thighs and leave at ¼-inch to shrink.
2. Carefully peel off the skin and remove large deposits of fat under the skin and behind the thighs.
3. Lightly rub olive oil behind and below the skin and thighs. A seasoning from Tuscan, seasoned on the skin of the thigh and the top and bottom of the back.
4. Wrap chicken thighs in plastic wrap, refrigerate for 1–2 hours and allow time for flavor to be absorbed before roasting.
5. Set the wood pellet smoker grill for indirect cooking and use the pellets to preheat to 375°F.
6. Roast for 40–60 minutes until the internal temperature of the thick part of the chicken thigh reaches 180°F.
7. Place the roasted Tuscan thighs under a loose foil tent for 15 minutes before serving.

NUTRITION:

Calories: 177
Fat: 8 g.
Protein: 25 g.

74. TERIYAKI SMOKED DRUMSTICK

PREPARATION TIME:	COOKING TIME:	SERVINGS:
15'	1 h 30'	4

INGREDIENTS:

3 cup teriyaki marinade and cooking sauce like Yoshida's® original gourmet
3 tsps. poultry seasoning
1 tsp. garlic powder
10 chicken drumsticks

DIRECTIONS:

1. In a medium bowl, mix the marinade and cooking sauce with the chicken seasoning and garlic powder.
2. Peel off the skin of the drumsticks to promote marinade penetration.
3. Put the drumsticks in a marinade pan or 1-gallon plastic sealable bag, and pour the marinade mixture into the drumsticks. Refrigerate overnight.
4. Rotate the chicken leg in the morning.
5. Configure a wood pellet smoking grill for indirect cooking.
6. Place the skin on the drumstick and, while the grill is preheating, hang the drumsticks on a poultry leg and wing rack to drain the cooking sheet on the counter. If you do not have a poultry leg and feather rack, you can dry the drumstick by tapping it with a paper towel.
7. Preheat wood pellet smoker grill to 180ºF using hickory or maple pellets.
8. Make marinate the drumsticks for 1 hour.
9. After 1 hour, raise the whole temperature to 350°F and cook the drumsticks for another 30-45 minutes until the thickest part of the sticks reaches an internal temperature of 180°F.
10. Place the chicken drumsticks under the loose foil tent for 15 minutes before serving.

NUTRITION:

Calories: 340
Fat: 9 g.
Carbs: 16 g.
Protein: 45 g.

75. LEMON CORNISH CHICKEN STUFFED WITH CRAB MEAT

PREPARATION TIME:	COOKING TIME:	SERVINGS:
30'	1 h 30'	2-4

INGREDIENTS:

2 (about 1 ¾ lb. each) Cornish chickens
Half lemon
4 tbsps. western rub or poultry rub
2 cups stuffed with crab meat

DIRECTIONS:

1. Rinse chicken thoroughly inside and outside, tap lightly and let it dry.
2. Carefully loosen the skin on the chest and legs. Rub the lemon under and over the skin and into the cavity. Rub the western rub under and over the skin on the chest and legs. Carefully return the skin to its original position.
3. Wrap the Cornish hen in plastic wrap and refrigerate for 2–3 hours until the flavor is absorbed.
4. Prepare crab meat stuffing. Make sure it is completely cooled before packing the chicken. Loosely fill the cavities of each hen with crab filling.
5. Tie the Cornish chicken legs with a butcher's leash to put the filling.
6. Set wood pellet smoker grill for indirect cooking and preheat to 375°F with pellets.
7. Place the stuffed animal on the rack in the baking dish. If you do not have a rack that is small enough to fit, you can also place the chicken directly on the baking dish.
8. Roast the chicken at 375°F until the inside temperature of the thickest part of the chicken breast reaches 170°F, the thigh reaches 180ºF, and the juice is clear.
9. Test the crab meat stuffing to see if the temperature has reached 165°F.
10. Place the roasted chicken under a loose foil tent for 15 minutes before serving.

NUTRITION:

Calories: 660
Fat: 47 g.
Protein: 57 g.

76. FLATTENED MOJO CHICKEN

PREPARATION TIME:
25'

COOKING TIME:
1 h

SERVINGS:
12

INGREDIENTS:

3–4 lbs. whole chickens
3 tbsps. olive oil
6 cups Traditional Cuban Mojo
3 tsps. sea salt
3 tbsps. Adobo Criollo spices

DIRECTIONS:

1. Rinse chicken with cold water and pat dry. Cut out the backbone with kitchen shears.
2. Turn chicken breast side up and open like a book. Press down firmly on the breast to flatten and break rib bones. Loosen skin from the body under the breast and thighs.
3. Place each chicken in a gallon-size resealable bag with 6 cups Mojo. Marinate (flat) in refrigerator 24 hours. Remove chickens from bags and discard mojo.
4. Blot each bird dry, and rub each with 3 tsp. salt, 1 tbsp. olive oil, and then 1 tbsp. Adobo Criollo spice blend.
5. Preheat one side of your pellet grill; and leave one side unlighted, cover and preheat for 20 minutes.
6. Place chicken skin side down in the middle of the grill with legs closest to the heat.
7. Watch carefully and turn over when the skin starts to brown. Turn and move chicken to the "cool" side and cover with a large disposable aluminum pan (a favorite restaurant trick.)
8. Cooking time will vary, depending on the fire and the size of the chicken.
9. Check the temperature at 20 minutes after turning. When the temperature in the thigh reaches 175ºF, remove from the heat and let sit, loosely covered for 15 minutes.

NUTRITION:

Calories: 160
Fat: 10 g.
Carbs: 1 g.
Protein: 20 g.

77. SIZZLING' BUFFALO WINGS

| PREPARATION TIME:
10' | COOKING TIME:
40' | SERVINGS:
8 |

INGREDIENTS:

36 chicken wings, separated
1 tbsp. vegetable oil
1 tsp. salt
1 cup all-purpose flour
1 ½ tbsp. white vinegar
¼ tsp. cayenne pepper
¼ tsp. garlic powder
1 tsp. Tabasco sauce
¼ tsp. Worcestershire sauce
¼ tsp. seasoned salt
6 tbsps. Frank's® Red-Hot Sauce
6 tbsps. unsalted butter
Celery sticks blue cheese dressing

DIRECTIONS:

1. Mix all except chicken, salt, oil, and flour in a pan. Bring to a simmer, stirring, and then cool.
2. Toss the wings with oil, and salt. Place into a large plastic bag, add the flour, and shake to coat evenly. Remove from the bag, shaking off excess flour.
3. Place wings on a hot pellet grill, turning several times until golden brown.
4. Remove wings from the grill and place them in a sealed bowl with the sauce and shake well.
5. Serve immediately with blue cheese and chilled celery sticks.

NUTRITION:

Calories: 130
Fat: 6 g.
Carbs: 6 g.
Protein: 10 g.

78. PEANUT CHICKEN SATAY

PREPARATION TIME:
20'

COOKING TIME:
40'

SERVINGS:
8

INGREDIENTS:

4 tbsps. olive oil
4 tbsps. sesame oil
2 tsps. ginger powder
2 tsps. garlic powder
2 tbsps. curry powder
Butter lettuce leaves and fresh cilantro leaves needed
20 wooden skewers, soaked
2 lbs. chicken thighs, cut into strips
For the peanut sauce:
2 cups chunky peanut butter
½ cups soy sauce
¼ cup brown sugar
¼ cup sweet chili paste
1/3 cup limes juice
2/3 cup hot water

DIRECTIONS:

1. Combine oils, ginger, garlic, and curry powder in a shallow mixing bowl. Place the chicken strips in the marinade and gently toss until well coated.
2. Cover and let the chicken marinate in the refrigerator overnight.
3. Thread the chicken pieces onto the soaked skewers working the skewer in and out of the meat, down the middle of the piece, so that it stays in place during grilling.
4. Brush the pellet grill with oil to prevent the meat from sticking. Grill the satays for 3–5 minutes on each side, until nicely seared and cooked through.
5. Serve on a platter lined with lettuce leaves and cilantro; accompanied by a small bowl of peanut sauce on the side.
6. To make the sauce, combine the peanut butter, soy sauce, chili paste, brown sugar, and lime juice in a food processor or blender. Puree to combine, and drizzle in the hot water to thin out the sauce.
7. Pour the sauce into individual serving bowls.

NUTRITION:
Calories: 185
Fat: 9 g.
Carbs: 5 g.
Protein: 20 g.

79. SMOKED CHICKEN IN MAPLE FLAVOR

PREPARATION TIME:	COOKING TIME:	SERVINGS:
30'	6 h	1

INGREDIENTS:

5 lbs. (2.3 kg.) chicken breast, boneless

For the spice:
1 tbsp. chipotle powder
1 ½ tsp. salt
2 tsps. garlic powder
2 tsps. onion powder
1 tsp. pepper

For the glaze:
½ cup maple syrup
For the fire:
Preheat the smoker 1 hour before smoking.
Use charcoal and maple wood chips for smoking.

DIRECTIONS:

1. Preheat a smoker to 225°F (107°C) with charcoal and maple wood chips.
2. Place chipotle, salt, garlic powder, onion powder, and pepper in a bowl then mix to combine.
3. Rub the chicken with the spice mixture then place it on the smoker's rack.
4. Smoke the chicken for 4 hours and brush with maple syrup once every hour.
5. When the internal temperature has reached 160°F (71°C), remove the smoked chicken breast from the smoker and transfer it to a serving dish.
6. Serve and enjoy right away.

NUTRITION:
Carbohydrates: 27 g.
Protein: 19 g.
Sodium: 65 mg.
Cholesterol: 49 mg.

80. SOUTH-EAST-ASIAN CHICKEN DRUMSTICKS

PREPARATION TIME:	COOKING TIME:	SERVINGS:
15'	2 h	6

INGREDIENTS:

1 cup fresh orange juice
¼ cup honey
2 tbsps. sweet chili sauce
2 tbsps. hoisin sauce
2 tbsps. fresh ginger, grated finely
2 tbsps. garlic, minced
1 tsp. Sriracha
½ tsp. sesame oil
6 chicken drumsticks

DIRECTIONS:

1. Set the temperature of the grill to 225°F and preheat with a closed lid for 15 minutes, using charcoal.
2. Mix all the ingredients except for chicken drumsticks and mix until well combined.
3. Set aside half of the honey mixture in a small bowl.
4. In the bowl of the remaining sauce, add drumsticks and mix well.
5. Arrange the chicken drumsticks onto the grill and cook for about 2 hours, basting with remaining sauce occasionally.
6. Serve hot.

NUTRITION:

Calories: 385
Carbohydrates: 22.7 g.
Protein: 47.6 g.
Fat: 10.5 g.

81. GAME DAY CHICKEN DRUMSTICKS

PREPARATION TIME:	COOKING TIME:	SERVINGS:
15'	1 h	8

INGREDIENTS:

For the brine:
½ cup brown sugar
½ cup kosher salt
5 cup water
2 (12 oz.) bottles of beer
8 chicken drumsticks

For the coating:
¼ cup olive oil
½ cup BBQ rub
1 tbsp. fresh parsley, minced
1 tbsp. fresh chives, minced
¾ cup BBQ sauce
¼ cup beer

DIRECTIONS:

1. To make the brine, in a bucket, dissolve brown sugar and kosher salt in water and beer.
2. Place the chicken drumsticks in brine and refrigerate, covered for about 3 hours.
3. Set the temperature of the grill to 275°F and preheat with a closed lid for 15 minutes.
4. Remove chicken drumsticks from brine and rinse under cold running water.
5. With paper towels, pat dry chicken drumsticks.
6. Coat drumsticks with olive oil and rub with BBQ rub evenly.
7. Sprinkle the drumsticks with parsley and chives.
8. Arrange the chicken drumsticks onto the grill and cook for about 45 minutes.
9. Meanwhile, in a bowl, mix BBQ sauce and beer.
10. Remove from grill and coat the drumsticks with BBQ sauce evenly.
11. Cook for about 15 minutes more.
12. Serve immediately.

NUTRITION:
Calories: 448
Carbohydrates: 20.5 g.
Protein: 47.2 g.
Fat: 16.1 g.

82. CAJUN CHICKEN BREASTS

PREPARATION TIME:
10'

COOKING TIME:
6 h

SERVINGS:
6

INGREDIENTS:

2 lbs. chicken breasts, skinless, boneless
2 tbsps. Cajun seasoning
1 cup BBQ sauce

NUTRITION:

Calories: 252   Protein: 33.8 g.
Carbohydrates: Fat: 5.5 g.
15.1 g.

DIRECTIONS:

1. Set the temperature of the grill to 225°F and preheat with a closed lid for 15 minutes.
2. Rub the chicken breasts with Cajun seasoning generously.
3. Put the chicken breasts onto the grill and cook for about 4–6 hours.
4. During the last hour of cooking, coat the breasts with BBQ sauce twice.
5. Serve hot.

83. BBQ SAUCE SMOTHERED CHICKEN BREASTS

PREPARATION TIME:
15'

COOKING TIME:
30'

SERVINGS:
4

INGREDIENTS:

1 tsp. garlic, crushed
¼ cup olive oil
1 tbsp. Worcestershire sauce
1 tbsp. sweet mesquite seasoning
4 chicken breasts
2 tbsps. regular BBQ sauce
2 tbsps. spicy BBQ sauce
2 tbsps. honey bourbon BBQ sauce

NUTRITION:

Calories: 421   Protein: 41.2 g.
Carbohydrates: Fat: 23.3 g.
10.1 g.

DIRECTIONS:

1. Set the temperature of the Grill to 450°F and preheat with a closed lid for 15 minutes.
2. In a large bowl, mix garlic, oil, Worcestershire sauce, and mesquite seasoning.
3. Coat chicken breasts with seasoning mixture evenly.
4. Put the chicken breasts onto the grill and cook for about 20–30 minutes.
5. Meanwhile, in a bowl, mix all 3 BBQ sauces.
6. In the last 4–5 minutes of cooking, coat breast with BBQ sauce mixture.
7. Serve hot.

84. CRISPY & JUICY CHICKEN

PREPARATION TIME:
15'

COOKING TIME:
5 h

SERVINGS:
6

INGREDIENTS:

¾ cup dark brown sugar
½ cup ground espresso beans
1 tbsp. ground cumin
1 tbsp. ground cinnamon
1 tbsp. garlic powder
1 tbsp. cayenne pepper
Salt and ground black pepper, to taste
1 (4 lbs.) whole chicken, neck, and giblets removed

DIRECTIONS:

1. Set the temperature of the grill to 200–225ºF and preheat with a closed lid for 15 minutes.
2. In a bowl, mix brown sugar, ground espresso, spices, salt, and black pepper.
3. Rub the chicken with spice mixture generously.
4. Put the chicken onto the grill and cook for about 3–5 hours.
5. Remove chicken from grill and place onto a cutting board for about 10 minutes before carving.
6. Cut the chicken into desired sized pieces and serve.

NUTRITION:

Calories: 540
Carbohydrates: 20.7 g.
Protein: 88.3 g.
Fat: 9.6 g.

85. HOT AND SPICY SMOKED CHICKEN WINGS

PREPARATION TIME:	COOKING TIME:	SERVINGS:
30'	3 h	1

INGREDIENTS:

6 lbs. (2.7 kg.) chicken wings

For the rub:
3 tbsps. olive oil
2 ½ tbsp. chili powder
3 tbsps. smoked paprika
½ tsp. cumin
2 tsps. garlic powder
1 ¾ tsp. salt
1 tbsp. pepper
2 tsps. cayenne

For the fire:
Preheat the smoker 1 hour before smoking
Add soaked hickory wood chips during the smoking time

DIRECTIONS:

1. Divide each chicken wing into 2 then place in a bowl. Set aside.
2. Combine olive oil with chili powder, smoked paprika, cumin, garlic powder, salt, pepper, and cayenne then mix well.
3. Rub the chicken wings with the spice mixture then let them sit for about 1 hour.
4. Meanwhile, preheat a smoker to 225°F (107°C) with charcoal and hickory wood chips. Prepare indirect heat.
5. When the smoker is ready, arrange the spiced chicken wings on the smoker's rack.
6. Smoke the chicken wings for 2 hours or until the internal temperature of the chicken wings has reached 160°F (71°C).
7. Take the smoked chicken wings from the smoker and transfer them to a serving dish.
8. Serve and enjoy immediately.

NUTRITION:
Calories: 366
Carbohydrates: 17 g.
Protein: 29 g.

86. SWEET SMOKED CHICKEN IN BLACK TEA AROMA

PREPARATION TIME:
30'

COOKING TIME:
10 h

SERVINGS:
1

INGREDIENTS:

6 lbs. (2.7 kg) chicken breast

For the rub:
¼ cup salt
2 tbsps. chili powder
2 tbsps. Chinese 5-spice
1 ½ cups brown sugar

For the smoke:
Preheat the smoker 1 hour before smoking.
Add soaked hickory wood chips during the smoking time.
2 cups black tea

DIRECTIONS:

1. Place salt, chili powder, Chinese 5-spice, and brown sugar in a bowl then stir to combine.
2. Rub the chicken breast with the spice mixture then marinate overnight. Store in the refrigerator to keep it fresh.
3. In the morning, preheat a smoker to 225°F (107°C) with charcoal and hickory wood chips. Prepare indirect heat.
4. Pour black tea into a disposable aluminum pan then place in the smoker.
5. Remove the chicken from the refrigerator then thaw while waiting for the smoker.
6. Once the smoker has reached the desired temperature, place the chicken on the smoker's rack.
7. Smoke the chicken breast for 2 hours then check whether the internal temperature has reached 160°F (71°C).
8. Take the smoked chicken breast out from the smoker and transfer it to a serving dish.
9. Serve and enjoy immediately.

NUTRITION:
Calories: 411
Carbohydrates: 27 g.
Protein: 19 g.
Sodium: 65 mg.

87. SWEET SMOKED GINGERY LEMON CHICKEN

PREPARATION TIME:	COOKING TIME:	SERVINGS:
30'	6 h	1

INGREDIENTS:

2 (4 lbs./ 1.8 kg.) whole chicken
¼ cup olive oil

For the rub:
¼ cup salt
2 tbsps. pepper
¼ cup garlic powder

For the filling:
8 (1-inch each) fresh ginger
8 sticks cinnamon
½ cup lemon, sliced
6 cloves

For the smoke:
Preheat the smoker 1 hour before smoking.
Add soaked hickory wood chips during the smoking time.

DIRECTIONS:

1. Preheat a smoker to 225°F (107°C). Use soaked hickory wood chips to make indirect heat.
2. Rub the chicken with salt, pepper, and garlic powder then set aside.
3. Fill the chicken cavities with ginger, cinnamon sticks, cloves, and sliced lemon then brush olive oil all over the chicken.
4. When the smoker is ready, place the whole chicken on the smoker's rack.
5. Smoke the whole chicken for 4 hours then check whether the internal temperature has reached 160°F (71°C).
6. When the chicken is done, remove the smoked chicken from the smoker then let it warm for a few minutes.
7. Serve and enjoy right away or cut into slices.

NUTRITION:
Calories: 411
Carbohydrates: 27 g.
Protein: 19 g.
Sodium: 65 mg.

7
TURKEY RECIPES

88. APPLE-WOOD-SMOKED WHOLE TURKEY

PREPARATION TIME:	COOKING TIME:	SERVINGS:
10'	5 h	6

INGREDIENTS:

1 (10–12 lbs.) turkey, giblets removed
Extra-virgin olive oil, for rubbing
¼ cup poultry seasoning
8 tbsps. (1 stick) unsalted butter, melted
½ cup apple juice
2 tsps. sage, dried
2 tsps. thyme, dried

DIRECTIONS:

1. Supply your smoker with wood pellets and follow the manufacturer's specific start-up procedure. Preheat with the lid closed to 250°F.
2. Rub the turkey with oil and season with the poultry seasoning inside and out, getting under the skin.
3. In a bowl, combine the melted butter, apple juice, sage, and thyme to use for basting.
4. Put the turkey in a roasting pan, place it on the grill, close the lid, and grill for 5–6 hours, basting every hour until the skin is brown and crispy, or until a meat thermometer inserted in the thickest part of the thigh reads 165°F.
5. Let the turkey meat rest for about 15–20 minutes before carving.

NUTRITION:

Calories: 180
Carbs: 3 g.
Fat: 2 g.
Protein: 39 g.

89. SAVORY-SWEET TURKEY LEGS

PREPARATION TIME:
10'

COOKING TIME:
5 h

SERVINGS:
4

INGREDIENTS:

1-gallon hot water
1 cup curing salt (such as Morton® Tender Quick)
¼ cup light brown sugar, packed
1 tsp. freshly ground black pepper
1 tsp. cloves, ground
1 bay leaf
2 tsps. liquid smoke
4 turkey legs
Mandarin glaze, for serving

DIRECTIONS:

1. In a huge container with a lid, stir together the water, curing salt, brown sugar, pepper, cloves, bay leaf, and liquid smoke until the salt and sugar are dissolved; let come to room temperature.
2. Submerge the turkey legs in the seasoned brine, cover, and refrigerate overnight.
3. When ready to smoke, remove the turkey legs from the brine and rinse them; discard the brine.
4. Supply your smoker with wood pellets and follow the manufacturer's specific start-up procedure. Preheat with the lid closed to 225°F.
5. Arrange the turkey legs on the grill, close the lid, and smoke for 4–5 hours, or until dark brown and a meat thermometer inserted in the thickest part of the meat reads 165°F.
6. Serve with Mandarin Glaze on the side or drizzle over the turkey legs.

NUTRITION:

Calories: 190
Carbs: 1 g.
Fat: 9 g.
Protein: 24 g.

90. HOISIN TURKEY WINGS

PREPARATION TIME:	COOKING TIME:	SERVINGS:
15'	1 h	8

INGREDIENTS:

2 lbs. turkey wings
½ cup hoisin sauce
1 tbsp. honey
2 tsps. soy sauce
2 garlic cloves, minced
1 tsp. ginger, freshly grated
2 tsps. sesame oil
1 tsp. pepper or to taste
1 tsp. salt or to taste
¼ cup pineapple juice

For the garnish:

1 tbsp. green onions, chopped
1 tbsp. sesame seeds
1 lemon (cut into wedges)

DIRECTIONS:

1. In a huge container, combine the honey, garlic, ginger, soy sauce, hoisin sauce, sesame oil, pepper, and salt. Put all the mixture into a zip lock bag and add the wings. Refrigerate for 2 hours.
2. Remove turkey from the marinade and reserve it. Let the turkey rest for a few minutes, until it is at room temperature.
3. Preheat your grill to 300°F with the lid closed for 15 minutes.
4. Arrange the wings into a grilling basket and place the basket on the grill.
5. Grill for 1 hour or until the internal temperature of the wings reaches 165°F.
6. Meanwhile, pour the reserved marinade into a saucepan over medium-high heat. Stir in the pineapple juice.
7. Wait to boil then reduce heat and simmer until the sauce thickens.
8. Brush the wings with sauce and cook for 6 minutes more. Remove the wings from heat.
9. Serve and garnish it with green onions, sesame seeds, and lemon wedges.

NUTRITION:

Calories: 115
Fat: 4.8 g.
Carbs: 11.9 g.
Protein 6.8 g.

91. TURKEY JERKY

PREPARATION TIME:	COOKING TIME:	SERVINGS:
15'	4 h	6

INGREDIENTS:

For the marinade:
1 cup pineapple juice
½ cup brown sugar
2 tbsps. sriracha
2 tsps. onion powder
2 tbsps. garlic, minced
2 tbsps. rice wine vinegar
2 tbsps. hoisin
1 tbsp. red pepper flakes
1 tbsp. coarsely ground black pepper flakes
2 cups coconut amino
2 jalapeños (thinly sliced)

For the meat:
3 lbs. turkey breasts, boneless, skinless, sliced to ¼-inch thick

DIRECTIONS:

1. Pour the marinade mixture ingredients in a container and mix until the ingredients are well combined.
2. Put the turkey slices in a gallon-sized Ziploc® bag and pour the marinade into the bag. Massage the marinade into the turkey. Seal the bag and refrigerate for 8 hours.
3. Remove the turkey slices from the marinade.
4. Activate the pellet grill for smoking and leave the lid open for 5 minutes until the fire starts.
5. Close the lid and preheat your pellet grill to 180°F, using a hickory pellet.
6. Remove the turkey slices from the marinade and pat them dry with a paper towel.
7. Arrange the turkey slices on the grill in a single layer. Smoke the turkey for about 3–4 hours, turning often after the first 2 hours of smoking. The jerky should be dark and dry when it is done.
8. Remove the jerky from the grill and let it sit for about 1 hour to cool. Serve immediately or store in the refrigerator.

NUTRITION:
Calories: 109
Carbs: 12 g.
Fat: 1 g.
Protein: 14 g.

92. SMOKED WHOLE TURKEY

PREPARATION TIME:	COOKING TIME:	SERVINGS:
20'	8 h	6

INGREDIENTS:

3 gallons of water
1 (about 12–16 lbs.) whole turkey
1 cup rub your favorite
1 cup sugar
1 tbsp. garlic, minced
½ cup Worcestershire sauce
2 tbsps. canola oil

DIRECTIONS:

1. Thaw the turkey and remove the giblets.
2. Pour in 3 gallons of water in a non-metal bucket of about 5 gallons.
3. Add the BBQ rub and mix very well.
4. Add the garlic, the sugar, and the Worcestershire sauce; then submerge the turkey into the bucket.
5. Refrigerate the turkey in the bucket overnight.
6. Place the Grill on a HIGH SMOKE and smoke the turkey for about 3 hours.
7. Switch the grilling temp to about 350ºF; then push a metal meat thermometer into the thickest part of the turkey breast.
8. Cook for about 4 hours; then take off the wood pellet grill and let rest for about 15 minutes.
9. Slice the turkey, then serve and enjoy your dish!

NUTRITION:

Calories: 165
Fat: 14 g.
Carbs: 0.5 g.
Protein: 15.2 g.

93. SMOKED TURKEY BREAST

PREPARATION TIME:
10'

COOKING TIME:
1 h 30'

SERVINGS:
6

INGREDIENTS:

For the brine:
1 cup kosher salt
1 cup maple syrup
¼ cup brown sugar
¼ cup whole black peppercorns
4 cups cold bourbon
1 ½ gallon cold water
1 (7 lbs.) turkey breast

For the turkey
3 tbsps. brown sugar
1 ½ tbsp. smoked paprika
1 ½ tsp. chipotle chili powder
1 ½ tsp. garlic powder
1 ½ tsp. salt
1 ½ tsp. black pepper
1 tsp. onion powder
½ tsp. ground cumin
6 tbsps. unsalted butter, melted

DIRECTIONS:

1. Before beginning; make sure that the bourbon and the water are all cold.
2. Now to make the brine, combine the salt, the syrup, the sugar, the peppercorns, the bourbon, and the water in a large bucket.
3. Remove any pieces that are left on the turkey, like the neck or the giblets.
4. Refrigerate the turkey meat in the brine for about 8–12 hours in a resealable bag.
5. Remove the turkey breast from the brine and pat dry with clean paper towels; then place it over a baking sheet and refrigerate for about 1 hour.
6. Preheat your pellet smoker to about 300°F; making sure to add the wood chips to the burner.
7. In a bowl, mix the paprika with the sugar, the chili powder, the garlic powder, the salt, the pepper, the onion powder, and the cumin, mixing very well to combine.
8. Carefully lift the skin of the turkey; then rub the melted butter over the meat.
9. Rub the spice over the meat very well and over the skin.
10. Smoke the turkey breast for about 1 ½ hour at a temperature of about 375°F.

NUTRITION:
Calories: 94
Fat: 2 g.
Carbs: 1 g.
Protein: 18 g.

94. WHOLE TURKEY

PREPARATION TIME:	COOKING TIME:	SERVINGS:
10'	7 h 30'	10

INGREDIENTS:

1 frozen whole turkey, giblets removed, thawed
2 tbsps. orange zest
2 tbsps. fresh parsley, chopped
1 tsp. salt
2 tbsps. fresh rosemary, chopped
1 tsp. ground black pepper
2 tbsps. fresh sage, chopped
1 cup butter, unsalted, softened, divided
2 tbsps. fresh thyme, chopped
½ cup water
14.5 oz. chicken broth

DIRECTIONS:

1. Open the smoker hopper, add dry pallets, make sure the ash-can is in place, then open the ash damper, power on the smoker, and close the ash damper.
2. Set the temperature of the smoker to 180°F, let preheat for 30 minutes or until the green light on the dial blinks that indicate the smoker has reached to set temperature.
3. Meanwhile, prepare the turkey and for this, tuck its wings under it by using kitchen twine.
4. Place ½ cup butter in a bowl, add thyme, parsley, sage, orange zest, and rosemary, stir well until combined, and then brush this mixture generously on the inside and outside of the turkey and season the external of turkey with salt and black pepper.
5. Place turkey on a roasting pan, breast side up, pour in broth and water, add the remaining butter in the pan, then place the pan on the smoker grill and shut with lid.
6. Smoke the turkey for 3 hours, then increase the temperature to 350°F and continue to smoke for 4 hours or until thoroughly cooked and the internal temperature of the turkey reaches 165°F.
7. Basting the turkey with the dripping every 30 minutes, but not in the last hour.
8. When you are done, take off the roasting pan from the smoker and let the turkey rest for 20 minutes.
9. Carve turkey into pieces and serve.

NUTRITION:

Calories: 146
Fat: 8 g.
Protein: 18 g.
Carbs: 1 g.

95. HERBED TURKEY BREAST

PREPARATION TIME:
8 h 10'

COOKING TIME:
10'

SERVINGS:
2

INGREDIENTS:

7 lbs. turkey breast, bone-in, skin-on,
fat trimmed
¾ cup salt
1/3 cup brown sugar
4 quarts water cold
For herbed butter:
1 tbsp. parsley, chopped
½ tsp. ground black pepper
8 tbsps. butter, unsalted, softened
1 tbsp. sage, chopped
½ tbsp. garlic, minced
1 tbsp. rosemary, chopped
1 tsp. lemon zest
1 tbsp. oregano, chopped
1 tbsp. lemon juice

NUTRITION:
Calories: 97
Fat: 4 g.
Protein: 13 g.
Carbs: 1 g.

DIRECTIONS:

1. Prepare the brine and for this, pour water in a large container, add salt and sugar and stir well until salt and sugar have completely dissolved.
2. Add turkey breast in the brine, cover with the lid and let soak in the refrigerator for a minimum of 8 hours.
3. Then remove turkey breast from the brine, rinse well and pat dry with paper towels.
4. Open the smoker hopper, add dry pallets, make sure the ash-can is in place, then open the ash damper, power on the smoker, and close the ash damper.
5. Set the temperature of the smoker to 350ºF, let preheat for 30 minutes or until the green light on the dial blinks that indicate the smoker has reached to set temperature.
6. Meanwhile, take a roasting pan, pour in 1 cup water, then place a wire rack in it and place turkey breast on it.
7. Prepare the herb butter and for this, place butter in a heatproof bowl, add remaining ingredients for the butter and stir until just mix.
8. Loosen the skin of the turkey from its breast by using your fingers, then insert 2 tbsps. of prepared herb butter on each side of the skin of the breastbone and spread it evenly, pushing out all the air pockets.
9. Place the remaining herb butter in the bowl into the microwave wave and heat for 1 minute or more at a HIGH HEAT setting or until melted.
10. Then brush melted herb butter on the outside of the turkey breast and place roasting pan containing turkey on the smoker grill.
11. Shut the smoker with lid and smoke for 2 hours and 30 minutes or until the turkey breast is nicely golden brown and the internal temperature of the turkey reaches 165ºF, flipping the turkey and basting with melted herb butter after 1 hour and 30 minutes smoking.
12. When done, transfer the turkey breast to a cutting board, let it rest for 15 minutes, then carve it into pieces and serve.

96. JALAPEÑO INJECTION TURKEY

PREPARATION TIME: 15'	COOKING TIME: 4 h 10'	SERVINGS: 4

INGREDIENTS:

15 lbs. whole turkey, giblet removed
½ medium red onion, peeled and minced
8 jalapeño peppers
2 tbsps. garlic, minced
4 tbsps. garlic powder
6 tbsps. Italian seasoning
1 cup butter, softened, unsalted
¼ cup olive oil
1 cup chicken broth

DIRECTIONS:

1. Open the smoker hopper, add dry pallets, make sure the ash-can is in place, then open the ash damper, power on the smoker, and close the ash damper.
2. Make the temperature of the smoker up to 200ºF, let preheat for 30 minutes or until the green light on the dial blinks that indicate smoker has reached to set temperature.
3. Meanwhile, place a large saucepan over medium-high heat, add oil and butter and when the butter melts, add onion, minced garlic, and jalapeño peppers and cook for 3–5 minutes or until nicely golden brown.
4. Pour in broth, stir well, let the mixture boil for 5 minutes, then remove the pan from the heat and strain the mixture to get just liquid.
5. Inject turkey generously with prepared liquid, then spray the outside of turkey with butter spray and season well with garlic powder and Italian seasoning.
6. Place turkey on the smoker grill, shut with lid, and smoke for 30 minutes, then increase the temperature to 325ºF and continue smoking the turkey for 3 hours or until the internal temperature of turkey reach 165ºF.
7. When done, transfer turkey to a cutting board, let rest for 5 minutes, then carve into slices and serve.

NUTRITION:

Calories: 131
Fat: 7 g.
Protein: 13 g.
Carbs: 3 g.

97. SMOKED TURKEY MAYO WITH GREEN APPLE

PREPARATION TIME:	COOKING TIME:	SERVINGS:
20'	4 h 10'	10

INGREDIENTS:

4 lbs. (1.8 kg.) whole turkey

For the rub:

½ cup mayonnaise
¾ tsp. salt
¼ cup brown sugar
2 tbsps. ground mustard
1 tsp. black pepper
1 ½ tbsp. onion powder
1 ½ tbsp. ground cumin
2 tbsps. chili powder
½ tbsp. cayenne pepper
½ tsp. old bay seasoning

For the filling:

3 cups green apples, sliced

DIRECTIONS:

1. Place salt, brown sugar, brown mustard, black pepper, onion powder, ground cumin, chili powder, cayenne pepper, and old bay seasoning in a bowl then mix well. Set aside.
2. Next, fill the turkey cavity with sliced green apples then baste mayonnaise over the turkey skin.
3. Sprinkle the dry spice mixture over the turkey then wrap with aluminum foil.
4. Marinate the turkey for at least 4 hours or overnight and store it in the fridge to keep it fresh.
5. On the next day, remove the turkey from the fridge and thaw at room temperature.
6. Meanwhile, plug the wood pellet smoker then fill the hopper with the wood pellet. Turn the switch on.
7. Set the wood pellet smoker for indirect heat then adjust the temperature to 275°F (135°C).
8. Unwrap the turkey and place it in the wood pellet smoker.
9. Smoke the turkey for 4 hours or until the internal temperature has reached 170°F (77°C).
10. Remove the smoked turkey from the wood pellet smoker and serve.

NUTRITION:

Calories: 340
Carbs: 40 g.
Fat: 10 g.
Protein: 21 g.

98. BUTTERY SMOKED TURKEY BEER

PREPARATION TIME:	COOKING TIME:	SERVINGS:
15'	4 h	6

INGREDIENTS:

4 lbs. (1.8 kg.) whole turkey

For the brine:
2 cans beer
1 tbsp. salt
2 tbsps. white sugar
¼ cup soy sauce
1-quart cold water

For the rub:
3 tbsps. unsalted butter
1 tsp. smoked paprika
1 ½ tsp. garlic powder
1 tsp. pepper
¼ tsp. cayenne pepper

DIRECTIONS:

1. Pour beer into a container then add salt, white sugar, and soy sauce then stir well.
2. Put the turkey into the brine mixture cold water over the turkey. Make sure that the turkey is completely soaked.
3. Soak the turkey in the brine for at least 6 hours or overnight and store it in the fridge to keep it fresh.
4. On the next day, remove the turkey from the fridge and take it out of the brine mixture.
5. Wash and rinse the turkey then pat it dry.
6. Next, plug the wood pellet smoker then fill the hopper with the wood pellet. Turn the switch on.
7. Set the wood pellet smoker for indirect heat then adjust the temperature to 275°F (135°C).
8. Open the beer can then push it into the turkey cavity. Then, brush the rub mixture generously over the turkey.
9. Place the seasoned turkey in the wood pellet smoker and make a tripod using the beer can and the 2 turkey legs.
10. Smoke the turkey for 4 hours or until the internal temperature has reached 170°F (77°C).
11. Once it is done, remove the smoked turkey from the wood pellet smoker and transfer it to a serving dish.

NUTRITION:
Calories: 229
Carbs: 34 g.
Fat: 8 g.
Protein: 3 g.

99. BARBECUE CHILI SMOKED TURKEY BREAST

PREPARATION TIME:
15'

COOKING TIME:
4 h 20'

SERVINGS:
8

INGREDIENTS:

3 lbs. (1.4 kg.) turkey breast

For the rub:
¾ tsp. salt
½ tsp. pepper
½ tsp. garlic powder

For the glaze:
1 tbsp. olive oil
¾ cup ketchup
3 tbsps. white vinegar
3 tbsps. brown sugar
1 tbsp. smoked paprika
¾ tsp. chili powder
¼ tsp. cayenne powder

DIRECTIONS:

1. Score the turkey breast at several places then sprinkle salt and pepper over it.
2. Let the seasoned turkey breast rest for approximately 10 minutes.
3. In the meantime, plug the wood pellet smoker then fill the hopper with the wood pellet. Turn the switch on.
4. Set the wood pellet smoker for indirect heat then adjust the temperature to 275°F (135°C).
5. Place the seasoned turkey breast in the wood pellet smoker and smoke for 2 hours.
6. In the meantime, combine olive oil, ketchup, white vinegar, brown sugar, smoked paprika; chili powder, garlic powder, and cayenne pepper in a saucepan then stir until incorporated. Wait to simmer then remove from heat.
7. After 2 hours of smoking, baste the sauce over the turkey breast and continue smoking for another 2 hours.
8. Once the internal temperature of the smoked turkey breast has reached 170°F (77°C) remove it from the wood pellet smoker and wrap it with aluminum foil.
9. Let the smoked turkey breast rest for approximately 15–30 minutes then unwrap it.
10. Cut the smoked turkey breast into thick slices then serve.

NUTRITION:
Calories: 290
Carbs: 2 g.
Fat: 3 g.
Protein: 63 g.

100. HOT SAUCE SMOKED TURKEY TABASCO

PREPARATION TIME: 20'	COOKING TIME: 4 h 15'	SERVINGS: 8

INGREDIENTS:

4 lbs. (1.8 kg.) whole turkey

For the rub:
¼ cup brown sugar
2 tsps. smoked paprika
1 tsp. salt
1 ½ tsp. onion powder
2 tsps. oregano
2 tsps. garlic powder
½ tsp. thyme, dried
½ tsp. white pepper
½ tsp. cayenne pepper

For the glaze:
½ cup ketchup
½ cup hot sauce
1 tbsp. cider vinegar
2 tsps. tabasco
½ tsp. Cajun spices
3 tbsps. unsalted butter

DIRECTIONS:

1. Rub the turkey with 2 tbsps. of brown sugar, smoked paprika, salt, onion powder, oregano, garlic powder, dried thyme, white pepper, and cayenne pepper. Let the turkey rest for 1 hour.
2. Plug the wood pellet smoker then fill the hopper with the wood pellet. Turn the switch on.
3. Set the wood pellet smoker for indirect heat then adjust the temperature to 275°F (135°C).
4. Place the seasoned turkey in the wood pellet smoker and smoke for 4 hours.
5. In the meantime, place ketchup, hot sauce, cider vinegar, Tabasco, and Cajun spices in a saucepan then bring to a simmer.
6. Remove the sauce from heat and quickly add unsalted butter to the saucepan. Stir until melted.
7. After 4 hours of smoking, baste the Tabasco sauce over the turkey then continue smoking for 15 minutes.
8. Once the internal temperature of the smoked turkey has reached 170°F (77°C), remove it from the wood pellet smoker and place it on a serving dish.

NUTRITION:
Calories: 160
Carbs: 2 g.
Fat: 14 g.
Protein: 7 g.

101. CURED TURKEY DRUMSTICKS

PREPARATION TIME:
20'

COOKING TIME:
2-3 h

SERVINGS:
3

INGREDIENTS:

3 fresh or thawed frozen turkey
drumsticks
3 tbsps. extra-virgin olive oil

For the brine:

4 cups water, filtered
¼ cup kosher salt
¼ cup brown sugar
1 tsp. garlic powder
1 tsp. poultry seasoning
½ tsp. red pepper flakes
1 tsp. pink hardened salt

DIRECTIONS:

1. Put the brine ingredients in a 1-gallon sealable bag. Add the turkey drumsticks to the brine and refrigerate for 12 hours.
2. After 12 hours, remove the drumsticks from the brine, rinse with cold water, and pat dry with a paper towel.
3. Air-dry the drumstick in the refrigerator without a cover for 2 hours.
4. Remove the drumsticks from the refrigerator and rub a tbsp. of extra-virgin olive oil under and over each drumstick.
5. Set the wood pellet or grill for indirect cooking and preheat to 250ºF using hickory or maple pellets.
6. Place the drumsticks on the grill and smoke at 250°F for 2 hours.
7. After 2 hours, increase grill temperature to 325°F.
8. Cook the turkey drumsticks at 325°F until the internal temperature of the thickest part of each drumstick is 180°F with an instant reading digital thermometer.
9. Place the smoked turkey drumsticks under a loose foil tent for 15 minutes before eating.

NUTRITION:

Calories: 278
Carbs: 0 g.
Fat: 13 g.
Protein: 37 g.

102. TAILGATE SMOKED YOUNG TURKEY

PREPARATION TIME: 20'	COOKING TIME: 4 h 30'	SERVINGS: 6

INGREDIENTS:

1 fresh or thawed frozen young turkey
6 glasses extra-virgin olive oil with roasted garlic flavor
6 original Yang dry lab or poultry seasonings

DIRECTIONS:

1. Remove excess fat and skin from turkey breasts and cavities.
2. Slowly separate the skin of the turkey to its breast and ¼ of the leg, leaving the skin intact.
3. Apply olive oil to the chest, under the skin, and on the skin.
4. Gently rub or season to the chest cavity, under the skin, and on the skin.
5. Set up a tailgate wood pellet smoker grill for indirect cooking and smoking. Preheat to 225°F using apple or cherry pellets.
6. Put the turkey meat on the grill with the chest up.
7. Suck the turkey for 4 hours and 30 minutes at 225°F until the thickest part of the turkey's chest reaches an internal temperature of 170°F and the juice is clear.
8. Before engraving, place the turkey under a loose foil tent for 20 minutes

NUTRITION:

Calories: 240
Carbs: 27 g.
Fat: 9 g.
Protein: 15 g.

103. ROAST TURKEY ORANGE

PREPARATION TIME:
30'

COOKING TIME:
2 h 30'

SERVINGS:
-

INGREDIENTS:

1 frozen long island turkey
3 tbsps. Western seasoning
1 large orange, cut into wedges
3 celery stems, chopped into large chunks
½ small red onion

For the orange sauce:

2 cups orange
2 tbsps. soy sauce
2 tbsps. orange marmalade
2 tbsps. honey
3 tsps. grated raw

DIRECTIONS:

1. Remove the nibble from the turkey's cavity and neck and retain or discard it for another use. Wash the duck and pat some dry paper towels.
2. Remove excess fat from the tail, neck, and cavity. Use a sharp scalpel knife tip to pierce the turkey's skin entirely, so that it does not penetrate the duck's meat, to help dissolve the fat layer beneath the skin.
3. Add the seasoning inside the cavity with one cup of rub or seasoning.
4. Season the outside of the turkey with the remaining friction or seasoning.
5. Fill the cavity with orange wedges, celery, and onion. Duck legs are tied with butcher twine to make filling easier. Place the turkey's breast up on a small rack of shallow roast bread.
6. To make the sauce, mix the ingredients in the saucepan over low heat and cook until the sauce is thick and syrupy. Set aside and let cool.
7. Set the wood pellet smoker grill for indirect cooking and use the pellets to preheat to 350°F.
8. Roast the turkey at 350°F for 2 hours.
9. After 2 hours, brush the turkey freely with orange sauce.
10. Roast the orange glass turkey for another 30 minutes, making sure that the inside temperature of the thickest part of the leg reaches 165°F.
11. Place turkey under a loose foil tent for 20 minutes before serving.
12. Discard the orange wedge, celery, and onion. Serve with ¼ of turkey with poultry scissors.

NUTRITION:

Calories: 216
Carbs: 2 g.
Fat: 11 g.
Protein: 34 g.

104. THANKSGIVING DINNER TURKEY

PREPARATION TIME:
15'

COOKING TIME:
4 h

SERVINGS:
16

INGREDIENTS:

½ lb. butter, softened
2 tbsps. fresh thyme, chopped
2 tbsps. fresh rosemary, chopped
6 garlic cloves, crushed
1 (20 lbs.) whole turkey, neck, and giblets removed
Salt and ground black pepper to taste

DIRECTIONS:

1. Set the temperature of the grill to 300ºF and preheat with a closed lid for 15 minutes, using charcoal.
2. In a bowl, place butter, fresh herbs, garlic, salt, and black pepper and mix well.
3. Separate the turkey skin from the breast to create a pocket.
4. Stuff the breast pocket with a ¼-inch thick layer of the butter mixture.
5. Season turkey with salt and black pepper.
6. Arrange the turkey onto the grill and cook for 3–4 hours.
7. Remove the turkey from the grill and place it onto a cutting board for about 15–20 minutes before carving.
8. Cut the turkey into desired-sized pieces and serve.

NUTRITION:

Calories: 965
Carbohydrates: 0.6 g.
Protein: 106.5 g.
Fat: 52 g.

105. HERB ROASTED TURKEY

PREPARATION TIME:
15'

COOKING TIME:
3 h 30'

SERVINGS:
12

INGREDIENTS:

14 lbs. turkey, cleaned
2 tbsps. mixed herbs, chopped
Pork and poultry rub as needed
¼ tsp. ground black pepper
3 tbsps. butter, unsalted, melted
8 tbsps. butter, unsalted, softened
2 cups chicken broth

DIRECTIONS:

1. Clean the turkey by removing the giblets, wash it inside out, pat dry with paper towels, then place it on a roasting pan and tuck the turkey wings by tiring with butcher's string.
2. Switch on the grill, fill the grill hopper with hickory flavored wood pellets, power the grill on by using the control panel, select SMOKE on the temperature dial, or set the temperature to 325ºF and let it preheat for a minimum of 15 minutes.
3. Meanwhile, prepared herb butter and for this, take a small bowl, place the softened butter in it, add black pepper and mixed herbs and beat until fluffy.
4. Place some of the prepared herb butter underneath the skin of the turkey by using a handle of a wooden spoon, and massage the skin to distribute butter evenly.
5. Then rub the exterior of the turkey with melted butter, season with pork and poultry rub, and pour the broth in the roasting pan.
6. When the grill has preheated, open the lid, place roasting pan containing turkey on the grill grate, shut the grill, and smoke for 3 hours and 30 minutes until the internal temperature reaches 165ºF and the top has turned golden brown.
7. When done, transfer turkey to a cutting board, let it rest for 30 minutes, then carve it into slices and serve.

NUTRITION:

Calories: 154.6
Fat: 3.1 g.
Carbs: 8.4 g.
Protein: 28.8 g.

106. TURKEY LEGS

PREPARATION TIME:
10'

COOKING TIME:
5 h

SERVINGS:
4

INGREDIENTS:

4 turkey legs

For the brine:
½ cup curing salt
1 tbsp. whole black peppercorns
1 cup BBQ rub
½ cup brown sugar
2 bay leaves
2 tsps. liquid smoke
16 cups warm water
4 cups ice cubes
8 cups cold water

DIRECTIONS:

1. Prepare the brine and for this, take a large stockpot, place it over high heat, pour warm water in it, add peppercorn, bay leaves, and liquid smoke, stir in salt, sugar, and BBQ rub and bring it to a boil.
2. Remove pot from heat, bring it to room temperature, then pour in cold water, add ice cubes and let the brine chill in the refrigerator.
3. Then add turkey legs in it, submerge them completely, and let soak for 24 hours in the refrigerator.
4. After 24 hours, remove turkey legs from the brine, rinse well and pat dry with paper towels.
5. When ready to cook, switch on the grill, fill the grill hopper with hickory flavored wood pellets, power the grill on by using the control panel, select SMOKE on the temperature dial, or set the temperature to 250ºF and let it preheat for a minimum of 15 minutes.
6. When the grill has preheated, open the lid, place turkey legs on the grill grate, shut the grill, and smoke for 5 hours until nicely browned and the internal temperature reaches 165ºF. Serve immediately.

NUTRITION:
Calories: 416
Fat: 13.3 g.
Carbs: 0 g.
Protein: 69.8 g.

107. TURKEY BREAST

PREPARATION TIME:
12'

COOKING TIME:
8 h

SERVINGS:
6

INGREDIENTS:

For the brine:
2 lbs. turkey breast, deboned
2 tbsps. ground black pepper
¼ cup salt
1 cup brown sugar
4 cups cold water

For the BBQ rub:
2 tbsps. onions, dried
2 tbsps. garlic powder
¼ cup paprika
2 tbsps. ground black pepper
1 tbsp. salt
2 tbsps. brown sugar
2 tbsps. red chili powder
1 tbsp. cayenne pepper
2 tbsps. sugar
2 tbsps. ground cumin

DIRECTIONS:

1. Prepare the brine and for this, take a large bowl, add salt, black pepper, and sugar in it, pour in water, and stir until sugar has dissolved.
2. Place turkey breast in it, submerge it completely, and let it soak for a minimum of 12 hours in the refrigerator.
3. Meanwhile, prepare the BBQ rub and for this, take a small bowl, place all of its ingredients in it and then stir until combined, set aside until required.
4. Then remove turkey breast from the brine and season well with the prepared BBQ rub.
5. When ready to cook, switch on the grill, fill the grill hopper with apple-flavored wood pellets, power the grill on by using the control panel, select SMOKE on the temperature dial, or set the temperature to 180ºF and let it preheat for a minimum of 15 minutes.
6. When the grill has preheated, open the lid, place turkey breast on the grill grate, shut the grill, change the smoking temperature to 225ºF, and smoke for 8 hours until the internal temperature reaches 160ºF.
7. When done, transfer turkey to a cutting board, let it rest for 10 minutes, then cut it into slices and serve.

NUTRITION:
Calories: 250
Fat: 5 g.
Carbs: 31 g.
Protein: 18 g.

8
GAME RECIPES

108. AROMATIC SMOKED DUCK BREAST

PREPARATION TIME:
15' + marinate time

COOKING TIME:
3 h 10'

SERVINGS:
5

INGREDIENTS:

3 lbs. duck breast

For the marinade:
3 cups apple juice
1 tbsp. salt
1 ½ tbsp. sugar
2 tbsps. soy sauce
¾ tsp. paprika
¾ tsp. garlic powder
1 tsp. basil, dried
¾ tsp. pepper

DIRECTIONS:

1. Add apple juice into a container and season with salt, sugar, soy sauce, paprika, garlic powder, dried basil, pepper, and stir well.
2. Score duck breast at several places and put breast into the marinade. Marinate for 4 hours.
3. Pre-heat your smoker to 325ºF, remove the breast from marinade, and place in smoker
4. Smoke until the internal temperature reaches 325ºF.
5. Remove and cut smoked duck breast into thick slices, serve and enjoy!

NUTRITION:
Calories: 136
Protein: 7.48 g.
Fat: 2.82 g.
Carbohydrates: 20.42 g.

109. SMOKED QUAILS

PREPARATION TIME:
15' + marinate time

COOKING TIME:
1 h 10'

SERVINGS:
4

INGREDIENTS:

5 lbs. quails

For the marinade:
2 cups orange juice
1 cup soy sauce
2 tbsps. garlic, minced
½ cup brown sugar
¼ cup olive oil
1 tbsp. pepper
1 cup onion, chopped

DIRECTIONS:

1. Add orange juice into a container and add soy sauce, garlic, brown sugar, olive oil, pepper, onion, and stir well.
2. Add quails to the container and toss well to coat.
3. Cover the container with a lid and marinate the quails for 3 hours.
4. Marinate quails overnight.
5. Preheat your Smoker to 225ºF.
6. Add quails (breast side up) and smoke for 1 hour until internal temperature reaches 145ºF.
7. Once done, remove and serve.
8. Enjoy!

NUTRITION:
Calories: 417
Protein: 43.2 g.
Fat: 16.98 g.
Carbohydrates: 20.78 g.

110. SMOKED RABBIT

PREPARATION TIME:
15' + 60' marinate time

COOKING TIME:
2 h

SERVINGS:
5

INGREDIENTS:

1 cottontail rabbit, skinned and gutted
2 tbsps. salt
½ cup white vinegar
Water as needed

For the rub:

1 tbsp. garlic powder
1 tbsp. cayenne pepper
1 tbsp. salt
1 bottle BBQ sauce

DIRECTIONS:

1. Take a bowl and add in your kosher salt alongside the white vinegar to make your brine.
2. Pour the brine over your rabbit using a shallow dish and add just enough water to cover up the whole of your rabbit.
3. Let it sit for 1 hour.
4. Preheat your smoker to a temperature of 200ºF.
5. Take a bowl and whisk in the garlic powder, salt, BBQ sauce, and cayenne pepper to make the rubbing.
6. Season the rabbit nicely.
7. Toss your rabbit in your smoker and add the hickory wood to your wood chamber.
8. Let it smoke for 2 hours and keep adding wood pellets after every 15 minutes.
9. Remove the rabbit from your smoker and serve hot.

NUTRITION:

Calories 93
Protein: 3.31 g.
Fat: 0.3 g.
Carbohydrates: 19.44 g.

TTL CORNISH GAME HEN

PREPARATION TIME:
30'

COOKING TIME:
2-3 h

SERVINGS:
4

INGREDIENTS:

2 cornish game hens
Salt as needed
Fresh ground pepper as needed
1 cup quick-cooking rice, seasoned and browned
1 small onion, chopped
½ cup orange juice, squeezed
½ cup apricot jelly
1 tbsp. butter

DIRECTIONS:

1. Pre-heat your smoker to 275ºF.
2. Season the birds with pepper and salt.
3. Take a small saucepan over low heat and add 2 tbsps. of butter. Melt the butter and stir in rice and onion.
4. Stuff the hens with the rice mix and secure the legs with twine.
5. Rinse the saucepan and put it back to low heat.
6. Melt remaining 2 tbsps. of butter and stir in orange juice alongside apricot jelly.
7. Whisk until smooth.
8. Baste the hen with the jelly glaze.
9. Transfer the birds to your smoker and smoke for 2–3 hours until the internal temperature reaches 170ºF.
10. Brush with more jelly, and enjoy it!

NUTRITION:

Calories 232
Protein: 30.07 g.
Fat: 4.96 g.
Carbohydrates: 16.47 g.

112. SMOKED WHOLE DUCK

PREPARATION TIME:
15'

COOKING TIME:
2 h 30'

SERVINGS:
4

INGREDIENTS:

2 tbsps. baking soda
1 tbsp. Chinese 5-spice
1 duck, thawed
1 Granny Smith apple, cored and diced
1 orange, quartered and sliced
2 tbsps. chicken seasoning, divided

DIRECTIONS:

1. Start by washing the duck under cool running water from the inside and out; then pat the meat dry with clean paper towels.
2. Combine the chicken seasoning and the Chinese 5-spice; then combine with the baking soda for extra crispy skin.
3. Season the duck from the inside and out.
4. Tuck the orange and apple slices into the cavity.
5. Turn your wood pellet smoker grill to SMOKE mode; then let the fire catch and set it to about 300°F to preheat.
6. Place the duck on the grill grate or in a pan. Roast for about 2 ½ hours at a temperature of about 160°F.
7. Place the foil loosely on top of the duck and let rest for about 15 minutes.
8. Serve and enjoy your delicious dish!

NUTRITION:

Calories 310
Protein: 23.8 g.
Fat: 20.62 g.
Carbohydrates: 5.92 g

113. SMOKED VENISON

PREPARATION TIME:
10'

COOKING TIME:
2 h

SERVINGS:
4

INGREDIENTS:

1 lb. venison tenderloin
¼ cup lemon juice
¼ cup olive oil
5 garlic cloves, minced
1 tsp. salt
1 tsp. ground black pepper

DIRECTIONS:

1. Start by putting the whole venison tenderloin in a zip-style bag or a large bowl.
2. Add the lemon juice, olive oil, garlic, salt, and pepper into a food processor.
3. Process your ingredients until they are very well incorporated.
4. Pour the marinade on top of the venison; then massage it in very well.
5. Refrigerate and let marinate for about 4 hours or overnight.
6. When you are ready to cook, just remove your marinade's venison and rinse it off very well.
7. Pat the meat dry and let it come to room temperature for about 30 minutes before cooking it.
8. In the meantime, preheat your smoker to a temperature of about 225°F.
9. Smoke the tenderloin for about 2 hours.
10. Let the meat rest for 10 minutes before slicing it.
11. Top with black pepper; then serve and enjoy your dish!

NUTRITION:

Calories: 302
Protein: 34.42 g.
Fat: 16.24 g.
Carbohydrates: 3.36 g.

114. VENISON MEATLOAF

PREPARATION TIME:
20'

COOKING TIME:
1 h 30'

SERVINGS:
7

INGREDIENTS:

2 lbs. ground venison
1 onion, diced
1 egg, beaten
1 pinch salt
1 pinch pepper
1 tbsp. Worcestershire sauce
1 cup breadcrumbs
1 oz. packet onion soup mix
1 cup milk
Cooking spray

For the glaze topping:
¼ cup ketchup
¼ cup brown sugar
¼ cup apple cider vinegar

DIRECTIONS:

1. When you are ready to cook, start your wood pellet grill on smoke with the lid open for about 4–5 minutes.
2. Set the temperature to about 350°F and preheat with the lid close for about 10–15 minutes.
3. Spray a loaf pan with cooking spray; then, in a large bowl, combine the ground venison altogether with the onion, the egg, the salt, the pepper, and the breadcrumbs.
4. Add the Worcestershire sauce, the milk, and the onion soup packet, and be careful not to over mix.
5. In a small bowl, mix the ketchup, brown sugar, and apple cider vinegar.
6. Spread half of the glaze on the bottom and sides of a pan.
7. Add the meatloaf and spread the remaining quantity on top of the meatloaf.
8. Directly place on the smoker grill grate and smoke for about 1 hour and 15 minutes.
9. Let the meatloaf cool for several minutes before slicing it.
10. Serve and enjoy your dish!

NUTRITION:
Calories: 323
Protein: 29.33 g.
Fat: 12.7 g.
Carbohydrates: 23.61 g.

115. WOOD PELLET ELK JERKY

PREPARATION TIME:	COOKING TIME:	SERVINGS:
10'	6 h	10

INGREDIENTS:

4 lbs. elk meat
¼ cup soy sauce
¼ cup teriyaki sauce
¼ cup Worcestershire sauce
1 tbsp. paprika
1 tbsp. chili powder
1 tbsp. red pepper, crushed
3 tbsps. hot sauce
1 tbsp. pepper
1 tbsp. garlic powder
1 tbsp. onion salt
1 tbsp. salt
1 tbsp. olive oil

DIRECTIONS:

1. Start by mixing all of the ingredients and seasoning and the elk meat in a large bowl; then let sit in the refrigerator for about 12 hours.
2. Light your wood pellet smoker to a low temperature of about 160°F.
3. Take the elk meat out of your refrigerator and start making strips of the meat manually or with a rolling pin.
4. Add smoker wood chips to your wood pellet smoker grill and rub some quantity of olive oil over the smoker grate; layout the strips in one row.
5. Warm a dehydrator up about halfway during the smoking process.
6. Remove the elk jerky meat off your smoker at about 3 hours.
7. Line it into the kitchen.
8. Line your dehydrator with the elk jerky meat and keep it in for about 5–6 additional hours. Serve and enjoy!

NUTRITION:
Calories: 41
Protein: 1.39 g.
Fat: 1.39 g.
Carbohydrates: 6.23 g.

116. SPICED SMOKED VENISON TENDER

PREPARATION TIME:
20'

COOKING TIME:
7 h 10'

SERVINGS:
10

INGREDIENTS:

5 lbs. (2.3 kg.) venison

For the rub:
3 tbsps. black pepper
2 tbsps. paprika
1 ½ tbsp. kosher salt
1 tbsp. garlic powder
1 tbsp. onion powder
¾ tbsp. cayenne pepper
¾ tbsp. coriander
½ tbsp. dill

For the heat:
Use charcoal and alder wood chunks for indirect smokes.

For the water pan:
2 cups beef broth
½ tsp. ginger
1 lemongrass

DIRECTIONS:

1. Rub the venison with black pepper, paprika, kosher salt, garlic powder, onion powder, cayenne pepper, coriander, and dill.
2. Prepare the grill and set it for indirect heat.
3. Place charcoal and starters in a grill, then ignite the starters. Put the burning charcoal on one side of the grill.
4. Place a heavy-duty aluminum pan, then place it on the other side of the grill.
5. Pour beef broth into the aluminum pan, then add ginger and lemongrass to the broth.
6. Place wood chunks on top of the burning charcoal, then set the grill grate.
7. Cover the grill with the lid and set the temperature to 200°F (93°C).
8. Wait until the grill reaches the desired temperature, then place the seasoned venison on the grate inside the grill.
9. Maintain the heat and control the temperature. Add more charcoal and wood chunks if it is necessary.
10. Once the smoked venison's internal temperature has reached 160°F (71°C), remove it from the grill and transfer it to a serving dish. Serve and enjoy.

NUTRITION:
Calories: 30
Protein: 3.28 g.
Fat: 0.6 g.
Carbohydrates: 3.72 g.

117. CINNAMON SMOKED QUAILS ORANGE TEA

PREPARATION TIME:	COOKING TIME:	SERVINGS:
10'	1 h 10'	10

INGREDIENTS:

6 lbs. (2.7 kg.) quails

For the rub:
¼ cup Sichuan peppercorns
2 tbsps. kosher salt
1 tsp. orange zest, grated
1 tsp. ginger
1 cup tea leaves
1 cup brown sugar
1 tsp. cinnamon
2 cloves
¼ cup olive oil
3 tbsps. lemon juice

For the heat:
use charcoal and applewood chunks
for indirect smokes.
For the water pan:
2 cups orange juice

DIRECTIONS:

1. Combine Sichuan peppercorns with kosher salt, grated orange zest, ginger, tea leaves, brown sugar, cinnamon, and cloves.
2. Pour olive oil and lemon juice over the spice mixture, then stir until incorporated.
3. Rub the quails with the spice mixture and marinate for at least 3 hours. Store in the fridge to keep the quails fresh.
4. Prepare the grill and set it for indirect heat.
5. Place charcoal and starters in a grill, then ignite the starters. Put the burning charcoal on one side of the grill. Place a heavy-duty aluminum pan, then place it on the other side of the grill. Pour orange juice into the aluminum pan, then place wood chunks on top of the burning charcoal. Set the grill grate.
6. Cover the grill with the lid and set the temperature to 200°F (93°C).
7. Place the seasoned quails on the grate inside the grill, then smoke for 2 hours.
8. Once the smoked quails are done, or the smoked quail's internal temperature has reached 160°F (71°C), remove it from the grill and transfer it to a serving dish. Serve and enjoy.

NUTRITION:
Calories: 175
Protein: 2.12 g
Fat: 9.03 g.
Carbohydrates: 22.45 g.

118. SPICY AND HOT SMOKED RABBIT BARBECUE

PREPARATION TIME:	COOKING TIME:	SERVINGS:
20'	3 h 10'	10

INGREDIENTS:

6 lbs. (2.7 kg.) rabbit
For the brine:
2 tbsps. kosher salt
½ cup white vinegar
1-quart water
For the rub:
2 tbsps. garlic powder
1 tbsp. cayenne pepper
1 tbsp. kosher salt
1 tbsp. black pepper
For the glaze:
2 tbsps. garlic powder
2 tsps. jalapeño pepper, diced
1 tsp. cayenne pepper
2 tbsps. olive oil
2 cups ketchup
1 cup brown sugar
1 cup apple cider vinegar
½ cup apple juice
½ cup honey
1 tbsp. Worcestershire sauce
1 tsp. kosher salt
1 tsp. black pepper
For the heat:
Use charcoal and hickory wood chunks for indirect smokes.
For the water pan:
2 cups apple juice

NUTRITION:

Calories: 247   Carbohydrates:
Protein: 1.47 g.   57.38 g.
Fat: 2.99 g.

DIRECTIONS:

1. Pour water into a container, then stir in kosher salt and white vinegar.
2. Score the rabbit at several places, then put the rabbit into the brine. Soak the rabbit for at least 1 hour.
3. After 1 hour, take the rabbit out of the brine, then wash and rinse it. Pat the rabbit dry.
4. Prepare the grill and set it for indirect heat.
5. Place charcoal and starters in a grill, then ignite the starters. Put the burning charcoal on one side of the grill.
6. Place a heavy-duty aluminum pan, then place it on the other side of the grill.
7. Pour apple juice into the aluminum pan, then place wood chunks on top of the burning charcoal. Set the grill grate.
8. Cover the grill with the lid and set the temperature to 200°F (93°C).
9. Combine the rub ingredients—garlic powder, cayenne pepper, kosher salt, and black pepper in a bowl, then mix well.
10. Rub the rabbit with the spice mixture, then place it on the grate inside the grill. Smoke the seasoned rabbit for 3 hours.
11. Maintain the heat and control the temperature. Add more charcoal and wood chunks if it is needed.
12. Next, pour olive oil, ketchup, apple juice, apple cider vinegar, and honey into a bowl, then season with garlic powder, diced jalapeño pepper, cayenne pepper, and brown sugar, Worcestershire sauce, and salt, and pepper. Then stir until incorporated.
13. After 15 minutes of smoking, baste the rabbit with the glaze mixture and repeat once every 30 minutes.
14. Once the smoked rabbit is tender, and the smoked rabbit's internal temperature has reached 170°F (77°C), remove it from the grill.
15. Place the smoked rabbit on a serving dish and serve. Enjoy!

119. ROASTED VENISON TENDERLOIN

| PREPARATION TIME:
10' | COOKING TIME:
28' | SERVINGS:
6 |

INGREDIENTS:

2 (about 1 ½ lb. each) venison tenderloin

For the marinade:

¼ cup dry red wine
1 tsp. garlic, minced
2 tbsps. soy sauce
1 tbsp. rosemary, chopped
1 tsp. ground black pepper
½ cup olive oil

For the seasoning:

1 tbsp. salt
½ tbsp. ground black pepper

DIRECTIONS:

1. Before preheating the grill, marinate the venison.
2. For this, prepare the marinade; take a small mixing bowl and whisk garlic, wine, and soy sauce until combined.
3. Add black pepper and rosemary, stir until mixed, and then whisk in oil until emulsified.
4. Place venison in a large plastic bag, pour in prepared marinade, seal the bag, turn it upside down to coat venison and let it marinate in the refrigerator for a minimum of 8 hours.
5. Then remove the venison from the marinade, pat dry and then season with salt and black pepper.
6. When the grill has preheated, place venison on the grilling rack. Grill for 4 minutes per side until nicely browned, and then continue cooking for 20 minutes until the venison's internal temperature reaches 135ºF.
7. When done, let venison rest for 5 minutes, then cut into slices and serve immediately.

NUTRITION:

Calories: 182
Protein: 0.65 g.
Fat: 19 g.
Carbohydrates: 2.63 g.

120. CORNISH GAME HENS

PREPARATION TIME:	COOKING TIME:	SERVINGS:
20'	60'	4

INGREDIENTS:

4 game hens, giblets removed

For the rub:
4 tbsps. melted butter, unsalted
4 tsps. chicken rub

Other:
4 sprig rosemary

DIRECTIONS:

1. In the meantime, prepare hens and for this, rinse well, pat dry, then tuck their wings and tie their legs by using a kitchen string.
2. Then rub melted butter outside of hens, sprinkle with chicken rub, and then place a sprig of rosemary into the cavity of each hen.
3. When the grill has preheated, place hens on the grilling rack and grill for 1 hour or until the control panel shows 165ºF internal temperature, turning halfway.
4. When done, remove hens from the grill and let them rest for 5 minutes.
5. Serve immediately.

NUTRITION:
Calories: 276
Protein: 30.09 g.
Fat: 16.66 g.
Carbohydrates: 0.05 g.

121. DUCK BREASTS

PREPARATION TIME:	COOKING TIME:	SERVINGS:
10'	8'	3

INGREDIENTS:

3 duck breasts

For the rub:
3 oz. game rub

DIRECTIONS:

1. In the meantime, prepare the duck, and for this, season the bottom of each breast with the rub.
2. Score the top of each breast, season it with the remaining rub, and rest for 10 minutes.
3. When the grill has preheated, place duck breast on the grilling rack and grill for 4 minutes per side or until the control panel shows the internal temperature of 130ºF, turning halfway.
4. When done, remove the duck from the grill and let it rest for 10 minutes.
5. Then cut the duck breasts into slices and serve immediately.

NUTRITION:
Calories: 205
Protein: 33.08 g.
Fat: 7.08 g.
Carbohydrates: 0 g.

122. VENISON STEAKS

PREPARATION TIME:	COOKING TIME:	SERVINGS:
10'	26'	4

INGREDIENTS:

10 (6 oz.) venison steaks

For the marinade:
1 L. sprite, diet
6 oz. game rub

Other:
2 lbs. asparagus

DIRECTIONS:

1. Before preheating the grill, marinate the venison steaks and for this, take a container, pour in the sprite, and then stir in the game rub.
2. Add venison steaks and then let them marinate in the refrigerator for a minimum of 6 hours.
3. Then remove venison steaks from the marinade and pat dry.
4. When the grill has preheated, place steaks on the grilling rack and let smoke for 8 minutes per side or until the control panel shows the internal temperature of 125ºF.
5. When done, remove the steak from the grill and let it rest for 10 minutes.
6. Meanwhile, add asparagus to the grilling rack and cook for 10 minutes, turning halfway.
7. Then cut the steak into slices and serve with asparagus.

NUTRITION:
Calories: 156
Protein: 27.42 g.
Fat: 2 g.
Carbohydrates: 8.8 g.

123. MANDARIN GLAZED HENS

PREPARATION TIME:	COOKING TIME:	SERVINGS:
20'	40'	4

INGREDIENTS:

5 cornish game hens, giblets removed

For the rub:
2 tbsps. onion powder
1 tbsp. garlic powder
1 tbsp. ginger powder
1 tbsp. salt
2 tbsps. olive oil

For the stuffing:
16 sprigs thyme
2 orange, cut into quarters

For the glaze:
1 cup mandarin glaze

DIRECTIONS:

1. In the meantime, prepare hens.
2. Prepare the rub. Take a small bowl, place all of its ingredients in it, and stir until mixed.
3. Stuff each hen's cavity with 4 thyme sprigs and 1 wedge of orange, then sprinkle the exterior with the prepared rub.
4. Rub hens with oil and then tie the legs of hens with a kitchen string.
5. When the grill has preheated, place hens on the grilling rack and grill for 20 minutes.
6. Then brush hens with mandarin glaze, continue grilling for 20 minutes and then brush again with mandarin glaze.
7. Serve immediately.

NUTRITION:
Calories: 226
Protein: 25.84 g.
Fat: 10.98 g.
Carbohydrates: 4.76 g.

124. CAJUN CRAB STUFFED SHRIMP AND JICAMA CORN SALAD

PREPARATION TIME:	COOKING TIME:	SERVINGS:
20'	3-5'	4

INGREDIENTS:

Shrimp, stuffed
lump crab meat
red onion
garlic seasoning, minced
lime juice
lime zest
jalapeño
ritz crackers
bacon
red onion and jalapeño, grilled

DIRECTIONS:

1. Pick cartilage from the crab. Combine ingredients wrap with bacon. Grill till browned.
2. Remoulade mayo, chili sauce, tiger sauce, creole mustard, lemon juice, lemon zest, scallions, parsley, minced celery, minced garlic, salt, capers chopped, salt, black pepper. Combine all ingredients and chill Jicama corn salad.
3. We diced the corn on the cob, black beans, carrot, scallions, cilantro, basil, lime juice, lime zest, cumin red bell pepper, grill red peppercorn on the cob.
4. Rinse black beans. Combine ingredients and chill.

NUTRITION:

Calories: 94
Protein: 13.51 g.
Fat: 1.13 g.
Carbohydrates: 7.48 g.

125. CORNED BEEF PASTRAMI

PREPARATION TIME:	COOKING TIME:	SERVINGS:
5 h	**3 h**	**6**

INGREDIENTS:

1.5 lbs. coarse ground pepper
2 tbsps. garlic, granulated
2 tbsps. onion flakes
2 tbsps. ancho chili powder
1 cup Ancho espresso rub

DIRECTIONS:

1. Rinse the meat in chilly water and afterward absorb cold water for 24 hours, changing the water every 6 hours to pull a more incredible amount of the salt and fix it from the meat.
2. Remove from the water and pat dry with a towel. Apply the rub ingredients and put them in a safe spot while the smoker heats up. Cook at 250ºF until the inward temperature hits 150ºF. That should take 3–4 hours.
3. Wrap in either foil or butcher paper and keep cooking until the inner temp arrives 185–195ºF. That should take another 2 hours around.

NUTRITION:

Calories: 276
Protein: 20.39 g.
Fat: 19.76 g.
Carbohydrates: 3.65 g.

9
FISH RECIPES

126. BLACKENED SALMON

PREPARATION TIME:
10'

COOKING TIME:
30'

SERVINGS:
4

INGREDIENTS:

2 lbs. salmon fillets, scaled and deboned
2 tbsps. olive oil
4 tbsps. sweet dry rub
1 tbsp. cayenne pepper
2 garlic cloves, minced

DIRECTIONS:

1. Turn on your wood pellet grill. Set it to 350°F.
2. Brush the salmon with olive oil. Sprinkle it with the dry rub, cayenne pepper, and garlic.
3. Grill for 5 minutes per side.
4. Serving suggestion: Garnish with chopped parsley.

NUTRITION:

Calories: 220
Carbs: 1 g.
Fat: 13 g.
Protein: 23 g.

127. BLACKENED CATFISH

| PREPARATION TIME: | COOKING TIME: | SERVINGS: |
| 10' | 40' | 4 |

INGREDIENTS:

For the spice blend:

1 tsp. garlic, granulated
¼ tsp. cayenne pepper
½ cup Cajun seasoning
1 tsp. ground thyme
1 tsp. ground oregano
1 tsp. onion powder
1 tbsp. smoked paprika
1 tsp. pepper

For the fish:

4 catfish fillets
Salt to taste
½ cup butter

DIRECTIONS:

1. In a bowl, mix the ingredients for the spice blend.
2. Sprinkle both sides of the fish with the salt and spice blend.
3. Set your wood pellet grill to 450ºF.
4. Heat your cast iron pan and add the butter. Add the fillets to the pan.
5. Cook for 5 minutes per side.

NUTRITION:

Calories: 283
Carbs: 1 g.
Fat: 19 g.
Protein: 27 g.

128. SALMON CAKES

PREPARATION TIME:
10'

COOKING TIME:
30'

SERVINGS:
4

INGREDIENTS:

1 cup cooked salmon, flaked
½ red bell pepper, chopped
2 eggs, beaten
¼ cup mayonnaise
½ tbsp. dry sweet rub
1 ½ cups breadcrumbs
1 tbsp. mustard
2 tbsp. Olive oil

DIRECTIONS:

1. Combine all the ingredients except the olive oil in a bowl.
2. Form patties from this mixture.
3. Let sit for 15 minutes
4. Turn on your wood pellet grill.
5. Set it to 350ºF.
6. Add a baking pan to the grill.
7. Drizzle a little olive oil on top of the pan.
8. Add the salmon cakes to the pan.
9. Grill for 3–4 minutes.

NUTRITION:

Calories: 459
Carbs: 3 g.
Fat: 37 g.
Protein: 26 g.

129. SMOKED LEMON SALMON

PREPARATION TIME:
10'

COOKING TIME:
1 h 15'

SERVINGS:
4

INGREDIENTS:

2 lbs. salmon
6–8 slices lemon
Fresh dill, for serving

DIRECTIONS:

1. Set your wood pellet grill to 225ºF.
2. Add the salmon on top of a cedar plank.
3. Place the lemon slices on top.
4. Smoke for 1 hour.
5. Add the dill on top before serving.
6. Tip: You can also brine the salmon before cooking.

NUTRITION:

Calories: 125
Carbs: 1 g.
Fat: 2 g.
Protein: 26 g.

130. SMOKED SALMON

PREPARATION TIME:
10'

COOKING TIME:
1 h

SERVINGS:
6

INGREDIENTS:

1/3 cup olive oil
1 tsp. sesame oil
1/3 cup soy sauce
1 ½ tbsp. rice vinegar
1 tsp. garlic, minced
2 salmon fillets
1 tsp. onion salt
1 tsp. black pepper

DIRECTIONS:

1. Combine the olive oil, sesame oil, soy sauce, vinegar, and garlic in a bowl.
2. Add the salmon.
3. Marinate for 30 minutes. Turn on your wood pellet grill.
4. Let it fire up for 5 minutes while the lid is open. Set it to 225°F.
5. Add cedar planks to the grill.
6. Take the salmon out of the marinade.
7. Sprinkle both sides with onion salt and pepper.
8. Add the salmon fillets to the planks.
9. Grill for 30 minutes.
10. Let it rest before serving.

NUTRITION:

Calories: 132
Carbs: 0 g.
Fat: 8 g.
Protein: 14 g.

'B'L FISH TACOS

PREPARATION TIME:
0'

COOKING TIME:
30'

SERVINGS:
12

INGREDIENTS:

¼ tsp. cayenne pepper
½ tsp. cumin
1 ½ tsp. paprika
1 tsp. garlic powder
1 tsp. oregano, dried
Salt and pepper to taste
1 ½ lb. codfish
12 tortillas

For the toppings:
Salsa
Avocado, sliced
Sour cream

DIRECTIONS:

1. Preheat your wood pellet grill to 350ºF.
2. Combine the salt, pepper, herbs, and spices.
3. Sprinkle this mixture on both sides of the fish.
4. Grill the fish for 5 minutes per side.
5. Shred the fish with a fork.
6. Place on top of the tortillas.
7. Top with salsa, sour cream, and avocado.
8. Roll up the tortillas and serve.

NUTRITION:
Calories: 117
Carbs: 2 g.
Fat: 6 g.
Protein: 12 g.

132. HALIBUT WITH INDIAN RUB AND CORN SALSA

PREPARATION TIME:	COOKING TIME:	SERVINGS:
15'	30'	4

INGREDIENTS:

2 tsps. ground cumin
1 ½ tsp. turmeric
1 tsp. ground coriander
1 tsp. ground fennel seeds
Salt and freshly ground black pepper
4 fillets (Pacific salmon, (striped sea bass, hake fillets or their fillets fish can be substituted), 1-inch thick (2–2.5 lbs. total)
2 lemons juice
4 tbsps. ghee (refined at Indian and specialty stores) or refined butter; vegetable oil can be substituted
1 tbsp. fresh ginger, chopped
½ cup onions, finely chopped
1 cup fresh corn kernels, cooked (about 1 ear of corn)
2 tbsp. Oil for grill
1 tbsp. fresh cilantro leaves, chopped
1 cup water

DIRECTIONS:

1. Mix cumin, turmeric, coriander, fennel, ½ tsp. tsp. black pepper and ½ tsp. salt or taste. Rub the fish fillets on both sides with lemon juice, then rub with all but 2 tsps. of the spice mixture. Refrigerate for 3 hours.
2. While sea fish heat, put 2 tbsps. of ghee in a pan, add ginger and onions; then simmer until onions are browned.
3. Add the rest of the spice mixture and stew, stirring, until the spices are tender to the toast, then add the corn and lemon juice. Cook briefly and reserve.
4. Remove the fish from the refrigerator and coat it on both sides with the remaining 2 tbsps. butter.
5. Preheat the grill and oil it.
6. When hot, place the fish on the grill over charcoal over medium heat or gas fire and cook for about 5 minutes.
7. Use a spatula. Turn the fish over and grill for 4 minutes until some liquid begins to accumulate. A fish surface and a kitchen knife inserted just at the bone level can hold the meat away.
8. Salmon should be cooked for about 3 minutes on each side.
9. Remove fish on a hot plate or individual dishes.
10. Warm up the corn mixture, add cilantro, and a few tbsp. of water.
11. Pour corn over fish, garnish with lemon slices and serve.

NUTRITION:

Calories: 130
Carbohydrates: 5 g.
Protein: 79 g.
Cholesterol: 19 mg.

133. CHARRED STRIPED BASS NICOISE

PREPARATION TIME:
10'

COOKING TIME:
40'

SERVINGS:
4

INGREDIENTS:

3 tbsps. extra-virgin olive oil, plus more for the grill
2 garlic cloves, sliced
1 (2 lbs.) skin-on wild striped bass fillet (Pacific salmon, mahi-mahi, or barramundi may be substituted)
½ lemon juice
Salt and freshly ground black pepper to taste
2 medium ripe tomatoes, cut in ¼-inch-thick slices
12 oil-cured black olives, pitted, coarsely chopped
1 tbsp. fresh basil leaves, finely slivered
Aioli (optional)

DIRECTIONS:

1. In a saucepan, heat the oil, add the garlic, and cook over medium heat until golden brown. Remove from heat, strain the garlic, and chop.
2. Coat the fish with half the oil on both sides. Coat the side of the meat with lemon juice and season with salt and pepper.
3. To process the fish, you will need 2 large blades; if you don't have them, cut the steak in half or 4 pieces.
4. Coat tomato into slices and add the remaining oil.
5. Preheat the grill to very hot grills and oil.
6. Remove to a plate and cover with foil to stay warm.
7. Use the edge of the spatula to clean the grilles. Oil again.
8. Grill the fish, skin side up. Cook for about 5 minutes. Use the blades to rotate. Cook for 3 minutes on the skin until the skeleton inserted horizontally in the middle is hot. (Salmon needs less time.)
9. Transfer the fish to a hot plate and flatten the meat side with the tomatoes covered.
10. Sprinkle with olives, chopped garlic, basil, and serve with aioli aside, if you like.

NUTRITION:

Calories: 130
Carbohydrates: 5 g.
Protein: 79 g.
Cholesterol: 19 mg.

134. CHARCOAL-GRILLED STRIPED BASS

PREPARATION TIME:
10'

COOKING TIME:
30'

SERVINGS:
4

INGREDIENTS:

1 (3–4 lbs.) striped bass, gutted
Salt and freshly ground black pepper to taste
1 garlic clove, peeled
1 large sprig of fresh rosemary
1 bay leaf
1 tbsp. Oil
¼ lb. (1 stick) butter, melted and kept hot
¼ cup fresh parsley, chopped
Lemon wedges, for garnish

DIRECTIONS:

1. Prepare a charcoal fire. When white ash forms on top of coals, they are ready.
2. Meanwhile, prepare fish. Rub it inside and out with salt and pepper.
3. Cut a garlic clove into slivers.
4. Using a sharp paring knife, make a few small incisions along the backbone of the fish.
5. Insert slivers of garlic.
6. Place rosemary sprig and bay leaf in the cavity of the fish. Tie fish in 2 or 3 places with string to secure the cavity. Rub fish generously all over with oil. Place fish on hot grill and cook 10–15 minutes on one side, brushing occasionally with butter.
7. Using a pancake-turner or spatula or both, loosen fish from the grill and turn it to the other side.
8. Cook 10–15 minutes on that side, or until fish is done and flesh flakes easily when tested with a fork. Cooking time will depend on the size of fish, the intensity of heat, and how close fish is to coals.
9. Transfer fish to a hot platter and pour remaining butter over it. Sprinkle with parsley and garnish with lemon wedges.

NUTRITION:
Calories: 130
Carbohydrates: 5 g.
Protein: 79 g.
Cholesterol: 19 mg.

135. GREEK-STYLE FISH WITH MARINATED TOMATOES

PREPARATION TIME: 10'	COOKING TIME: 45'	SERVINGS: 4

INGREDIENTS:

2 cups your favorite Sun Gold cherry tomatoes, cut in half
4 tbsps. olive oil, or more as needed
2 tbsps. white wine vinegar
1 tbsp. chopped fresh hot peppers, such as jalapeño, or more to taste
1 fresh oregano cooker or 1 coffee stove
4 garlic cloves, sliced or more to taste
Salt and freshly ground black pepper to taste
1 large whole fish or 2 small fish (2–3 lbs. in total), such as striped sea bass, redfish, or trout; preferably butter and boneless, or simply emptied lemon sliced into noodles
4–6 sprigs of fresh thyme

DIRECTIONS:

1. Prepare the grill; the heat should be medium to high and about 4-inch from the fire.
2. Join in tomatoes, 2 tbsps. olive oil, vinegar, hot peppers, oregano, steam garlic slices, and a pinch of salt and pepper in a bowl; let them sit at room temperature for 30 minutes.
3. Then make a sharp blade of 3 or 4 parallel bars on each side of the fish, approximately at the bottom. Season the fish with salt.
4. Also, add the hot pepper, stuffed with garlic residue, a layer of lemon slices, and thyme twigs. On the outside, coat the fish with the remaining 2 tbsps. of oil and sprinkle salt and pepper.
5. Bake until firm enough to rotate, 5–8 minutes. Turn and cook the other side for 5–8 minutes. The fish is cooked when it is hot outside and the paddle is easy to pass through the meat.
6. Try the tomato mixture and change the spice, including more oil if needed. Serve fish garnished with tomatoes and their liquid.

NUTRITION:

Calories: 130
Carbohydrates: 5 g.
Protein: 79 g.
Cholesterol: 19 mg.

136. GRILLED FISH WITH AROMATICS

PREPARATION TIME:	COOKING TIME:	SERVINGS:
10'	50'	4

INGREDIENTS:

4 (1 kg.) salty guide, cod or snack or 1 (4–5 kg.) salmon, cleaned upside down

Vegetable oil for baking, scoops, and baking.

6 tbsps. extra-virgin olive oil

20 garlic cloves, peeled

12 twigs fresh thyme

12 sprigs of fresh rosemary

2 bay leaves

Salt and pepper to taste

1 cup water

NUTRITION:

Calories: 130
Carbohydrates: 5 g.
Protein: 79 g.
Cholesterol: 19 mg.

DIRECTIONS:

1. Rinse and dry the fish. Make 3 or 4 shallow cuts through the skin of the fish.
2. It may expand during cooking. Refrigerate in cool until ready.
3. Kindle and light a fire on the outdoor grill.
4. Preheat the oven to 300ºF.
5. When the coals are bright red and evenly dusted with ash, grill and allow to warm for 2–3 minutes. Grill well, using vegetable oil and paper toweling, being careful not to use so much oil that it will drip on coals and cause them to flame up.
6. Place the fish on the grill so that the steps below are perpendicular. Cook until fish has golden grill marks, about 3 minutes on each side. Using a metal spatula, lightly brush the vegetable oil into 1 or 2 greased baking dishes, depending on the amount of fish you are preparing.
7. Put them in the oven and bake until they are opaque; it will be about 12 minutes for small fish, 20–25 minutes for large fish.
8. About 10 minutes before the end, pour the fish 6 tbsps. of olive oil into a baking pan or mold and place in the oven to warm slightly.
9. On high heat, boil 2 cups of water at the bottom of the steam. Put the garlic cloves in the garlic, cover, and simmer until they are almost soft, about 8 minutes.
10. Add the remaining herbs to the steamer in an even layer, cover, and continue cooking for 3 minutes.
11. To serve, pour equal amounts of olive oil into the middle of hot dishes. If small fish are used, put them whole over the oil. If you are using large fish, such as salmon, remove the fillets and place the fillets of the same size in the oil.
12. Season to taste with thick salt and pepper.
13. Put the cooked herbs and garlic on one side of the plate and serve immediately.

137. BAKED FRESH WILD SOCKEYE SALMON

PREPARATION TIME:	COOKING TIME:	SERVINGS:
10'	40'	4

INGREDIENTS:

2 fresh wild sockeye salmon fillets, skin on
2 tsps. Seafood seasoning
¾ tsp. Old Bay seasoning

DIRECTIONS:

1. Flush the salmon fillets with cold water and pat them dry with a paper towel.
2. Delicately dust the fillets with the seasonings.
3. On the wood pellet smoker-grill
4. Arrange the wood pellet smoker-grill for non-direct cooking and preheat to 400°F utilizing any pellets.
5. Lay the salmon skin-side down on a Teflon-covered fiberglass tangle or directly on the grill grates.
6. Bake the salmon for 15–20 minutes, until the internal temperature arrives at 140°F, and additionally the substance chips effectively with a fork.
7. Rest the salmon for 5–6 minutes before serving.

NUTRITION:

Calories: 322
Carbs: 2 g.
Fat: 24 g.
Protein: 24 g.

138. ALDER CREOLE WILD PACIFIC ROCKFISH

PREPARATION TIME: 10'	COOKING TIME: 1 h 30'	SERVINGS: 4

INGREDIENTS:

4–8 (4–7 oz.) fresh wild Pacific rockfish fillets

3 tsps. roasted garlic–seasoned extra-virgin olive oil

2 tbsps. Creole Seafood Seasoning or any Creole seasoning

DIRECTIONS:

1. Rub the 2 sides of the fillets with olive oil.
2. Residue the 2 sides with the seasoning.
3. On the wood pellet smoker-grill
4. Design the wood pellet smoker-grill for non-direct cooking and preheat to 225°F utilizing birch pellets.
5. Place the fillets on a Teflon-coated fiberglass mat to keep them from adhering to the grill grates.
6. Smoke the fillets for approximately 1 hour and 30 minutes, until they arrive at an internal temperature of 140°F or potentially the flesh flakes easily with a fork.

NUTRITION:

Calories: 322
Carbs: 2 g.
Fat: 24 g.
Protein: 24 g.

139. ALDER WOOD-SMOKED BONED TROUT

PREPARATION TIME:
10'

COOKING TIME:
2 h

SERVINGS:
4

INGREDIENTS:

4 fresh boned entire trout, skin on and pin bones removed
5 cups Salmon and Trout Brine

NUTRITION:

Calories: 322
Carbs: 2 g.
Fat: 24 g.
Protein: 24 g.

DIRECTIONS:

1. Put the trout in a 2-liter plastic bag or on a brine rack. Place the bag on a shallow plate in case it spills and refrigerate for 2 hours, turning the trout on wheels to make sure it remains submerged. In case of spillage, place the bag on a shallow plate
2. Air-dry the brined trout in the refrigerator, uncovered, for 2 hours to enable the pellicle to frame.
3. Configure the wood pellet smoker-grill for non-direct cooking. On the off chance that your grill has cold-smoking capabilities, at that point configure your pellet smoker-grill for cold-smoking.
4. Preheat the grill to 190°F utilizing alder pellets. A pit temperature of 190°F should result in a cold-smoke temperature of 70–100°F in your smoker box, contingent upon the encompassing temperature.
5. Cold-smoke the trout for 90 minutes.
6. Following 90 minutes, move the cold-smoked boned trout to the wood pellet smoker-grill pit territory and increase the wood pellet smoker-grill temperature to 230°F.
7. Keep cooking the trout until the internal temperature of the trout at the thickest part arrives at 145°F.
8. Remove the trout from the grill and wait 5 minutes before serving.

Notes:

1. Search for boned trout in the fish department of your nearby supermarket, fish market, or even better, get your very own and remove every one of the bones yourself.
2. Boneless trout should be deboned, yet consistently take care of when eating fish.
3. Cold smoking happens at temperatures somewhere in the range of 70–100°F.

140. GARLIC SALMON

PREPARATION TIME:	COOKING TIME:	SERVINGS:
10'	45'	3

INGREDIENTS:

2 (12 oz.) salmon fillets
1/3 cup olive oil
1 tsp. parsley
1 tsp. garlic powder
2 tsps. seafood rub
5 lemon wedges, for serving

DIRECTIONS:

1. Preheat the grill on high until smoke is established.
2. Line a baking sheet with parchment paper.
3. Put salmon on baking sheet skin side down. Season the fillet with seafood rub.
4. Take a bowl, and combine olive oil, parsley, garlic, and set it aside for further use.
5. Brush the salmon with the mixture and transfer it to the baking sheet
6. Cook it over the grill grate for 15 minutes until the internal temperature reaches 140ºF.
7. At the end brush with an extra bowl mixture and serve with lemon wedges.

NUTRITION:

Calories: 322
Carbs: 2 g.
Fat: 24 g.
Protein: 24 g.

'141. PINEAPPLE MAPLE GLAZE FISH

PREPARATION TIME:
10'

COOKING TIME:
25'

SERVINGS:
3

INGREDIENTS:

3 lbs. fresh salmon
¼ cup maple syrup
½ cup pineapple juice

For the brine:

3 cups water
Sea salt, to taste
2 cups pineapple juice
½ cup brown sugar
5 tbsps. Worcestershire sauce
1 tbsp. garlic salt

DIRECTIONS:

1. Combine all the brine ingredients in a large cooking pan.
2. Place the fish into the brine and let it sit for 2 hours for marinating.
3. After 2 hours take out the fish and pat dry with a paper towel and set aside.
4. Preheat the smoker grill to 250ºF, until the smoke started to appear.
5. Put salmon on the grill and cook for 15 minutes.
6. Meanwhile, mix pineapple and maple syrup in a bowl and baste fish every 5 minutes.
7. Once the salmon is done, serve and enjoy.

NUTRITION:
Calories: 322
Carbs: 2 g.
Fat: 24 g.
Protein: 24 g.

142. SMOKED CATFISH

PREPARATION TIME:
10'

COOKING TIME:
15'

SERVINGS:
3

INGREDIENTS:

For the rub:
2 tbsps. paprika
¼ tsp. salt
1 tbsp. garlic powder
1 tbsp. onion powder
½ tbsp. thyme, dried
½ tbsp. cayenne pepper

Others:
2 lbs. fresh catfish fillets
4 tbsps. butter, soften

DIRECTIONS:

1. Take a mixing bowl, and combine all the rub ingredients in it, including paprika, salt, garlic powder, onion powder, thyme, and cayenne pepper.
2. Rub the fillet with the butter, and then sprinkle a generous amount of rub on top
3. Coat fish well with the rub.
4. Preheat the smoker grill at 200ºF for 15 minutes.
5. Cook fish on the grill for 10 minutes, 5 minutes per side.
6. Once done, serve and enjoy.

NUTRITION:
Calories: 222
Carbs: 2 g.
Fat: 14 g.
Protein: 25 g.

143. CLASSIC SMOKED TROUT

PREPARATION TIME:
10'

COOKING TIME:
40'

SERVINGS:
3

INGREDIENTS:

For the brine:
4 cups water
1–2 cups dark-brown sugar
1 cup sea salt

For the trout:
3 lbs. trout, backbone, and pin bones removed
4 tbsps. olive oil

DIRECTIONS:

1. Preheat the electrical smoker grill, by setting the temperature to 250ºF, for 15 minutes by closing the lid.
2. Take a cooking pot, and combine all the brine ingredients, including water, sugar, and salt.
3. Submerged the fish in the brine mixture for a few hours.
4. Afterward, take out the fish, and pat dry with the paper towel.
5. Drizzle olive oil over the fish, and then place it over the grill grate for cooking.
6. Smoke the fish, until the internal temperature reaches 140ºF, for 1 hour.
7. Then serve.

NUTRITION:
Calories: 222
Carbs: 2 g.
Fat: 14 g.
Protein: 25 g.

144. SMOKED SEA BASS

PREPARATION TIME:	COOKING TIME:	SERVINGS:
10'	40'	4

INGREDIENTS:

For the marinade:
1 tsp. blackened Saskatchewan
1 tbsp. fresh thyme
1 tbsp. fresh oregano
8 garlic cloves, crushed
1 lemon juice
¼ cup oil

For the sea bass:
4 sea bass fillets, skin off
1 cup Chicken rub seasoning
1 cup Seafood seasoning (like old bay)
8 tbsps. gold butter

For garnish:
Thyme
Lemon

DIRECTIONS:

1. Make the marinade: In a Ziploc® bag combine the ingredients and mix. Add the fillets and marinate for 30 min in the fridge. Turn once.
2. Preheat the grill to 325ºF with a closed lid.
3. In a dish for baking add the butter. Remove the fish from the marinade and pour it into the baking dish. Season the fish with chicken and seafood rub. Place it in the baking dish and on the grill. Cook 30 minutes. Baste 1–2 times.
4. Remove from the grill when the internal temperature is 160ºF.
5. Garnish with lemon slices and thyme. Enjoy!

NUTRITION:
Calories: 220
Protein: 32 g.
Carbs: 1 g.
Fat: 8 g.

145. SIMPLE AND DELICIOUS FISH

PREPARATION TIME:
45'

COOKING TIME:
10'

SERVINGS:
4-6

INGREDIENTS:

4 lbs. fish, cut it into pieces (portion size)
1 tbsp. garlic, minced
1/3 cup olive oil
1 cup soy sauce
Basil, chopped
2 lemons juice

DIRECTIONS:

1. Preheat the grill to 350ºF with a closed lid.
2. Combine the ingredients in a bowl. Stir to combine. Marinade the fish for 45 minutes.
3. Grill the fish until it reaches 145ºF internal temperature.
4. Serve with your favorite side dish and enjoy!

NUTRITION:
Calories: 153
Protein: 25 g.
Carbs: 1 g.
Fat: 4 g.

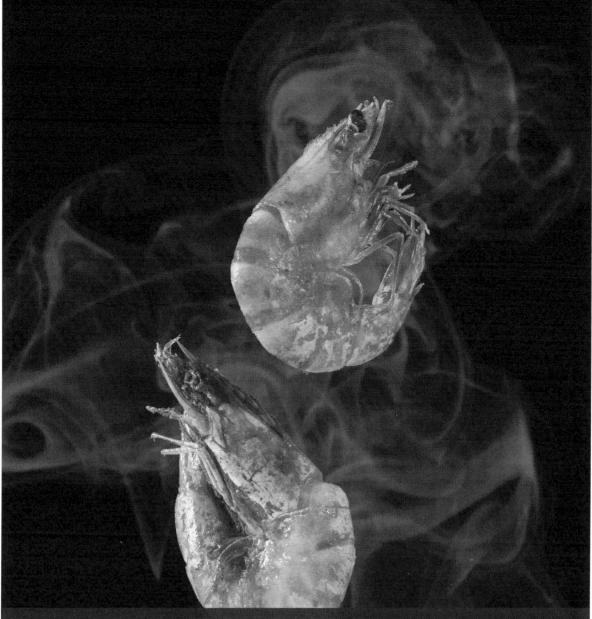

10
SEAFOOD RECIPES

146. BARBEQUE SHRIMP

PREPARATION TIME:
20'

COOKING TIME:
8'

SERVINGS:
6

INGREDIENTS:

2 lbs. raw shrimp, peeled and deveined
¼ cup extra-virgin olive oil
½ tsp. paprika
½ tsp. red pepper flakes
2 garlic cloves, minced
1 tsp. cumin
1 lemon juice
1 tsp. kosher salt
1 tbsp. chili paste
Bamboo or wooden skewers, soaked for 30 minutes, at least

DIRECTIONS:

1. Combine the pepper flakes, cumin, lemon juice, salt, chili, paprika, garlic, and olive oil. Add the shrimp and toss to combine.
2. Transfer the shrimp and marinade into a zip-lock bag and refrigerate for 4 hours.
3. Let shrimp rest at room temperature after pulling it out from the marinade.
4. Start your grill on SMOKE, leaving the lid open for 5 minutes, or until the fire starts. Use hickory wood pellet.
5. Keep lid unopened and preheat the grill to HIGH for 15 minutes.
6. Thread shrimps onto skewers and arrange the skewers on the grill grate.
7. Smoke shrimps for 8 minutes, 4 minutes per side.
8. Serve and enjoy.

NUTRITION:
Calories: 267
Fat: 11.6 g.
Carbohydrates: 4.9 g.
Protein: 34.9 g.

147. OYSTER IN SHELLS

PREPARATION TIME:	COOKING TIME:	SERVINGS:
25'	8'	4

INGREDIENTS:

12 medium oysters
1 tsp. oregano
1 lemon juice
1 tsp. freshly ground black pepper.
6 tbsps. unsalted butter, melted
1 tsp. salt or more to taste
2 garlic cloves, minced
2 ½ tbsp. Parmesan cheese, grated
2 tbsps. parsley, freshly chopped

DIRECTIONS:

1. Remove dirt.
2. Open the shell completely. Discard the top shell.
3. Gently run the knife under the oyster to loosen the oyster foot from the bottom shell.
4. Repeat steps 2 and 3 for the remaining oysters.
5. Combine melted butter, lemon juice, pepper, salt, garlic, and oregano in a mixing bowl.
6. Pour ½–1 tsp. of the butter mixture on each oyster.
7. Start your wood pellet grill on smoke, leaving the lid open for 5 minutes, or until the fire starts.
8. Keep lid unopened to preheat in the set HIGH with the lid closed for 15 minutes.
9. Gently arrange the oysters onto the grill grate.
10. Grill oyster for 6–8 minutes or until the oyster juice is bubbling and the oyster is plump.
11. Remove oysters from heat. Serve and top with grated Parmesan and chopped parsley.

NUTRITION:

Calories: 200
Fat: 19.2 g.
Carbohydrates: 3.9 g.
Protein: 4.6 g.

148. SMOKED SCALLOPS

PREPARATION TIME:	COOKING TIME:	SERVINGS:
10'	15'	6

INGREDIENTS:

2 lbs. sea scallops
4 tbsps. salted butter
2 tbsps. lemon juice
½ tsp. ground black pepper
1 garlic clove, minced
1 tsp. kosher salt
1 tsp. tarragon, freshly chopped

DIRECTIONS:

1. Let the scallops dry using paper towels and drizzle all sides with salt and pepper to season.
2. Place you are a cast iron pan in your grill and preheat the grill to 400°F with the lid closed for 15 minutes.
3. Combine the butter and garlic in a hot cast iron pan. Add the scallops and stir. Close grill lid and cook for 8 minutes.
4. Flip the scallops and cook for an additional 7 minutes.
5. Remove the scallop from heat and let it rest for a few minutes.
6. Stir in the chopped tarragon. Serve and top with lemon juice.

NUTRITION:

Calories: 204
Fat: 8.9 g.
Carbohydrates: 4 g.
Protein: 25.6 g.

149. CRAB STUFFED LINGCOD

PREPARATION TIME:
20'

COOKING TIME:
30'

SERVINGS:
6

INGREDIENTS:

For the lemon cream sauce:
4 garlic cloves
1 shallot
1 leek
2 tbsps. olive oil
1 tbsp. salt
¼ tbsp. black pepper
3 tbsps. butter
¼ cup white wine
1 cup whipping cream
2 tbsps. lemon juice
1 tbsp. lemon zest

For the crab mix:
1 lb. crab meat
1/3 cup mayo
1/3 cup sour cream
1/3 cup lemon cream sauce
¼ green onion, chopped.
¼ tbsp. black pepper
½ tbsp. old bay seasoning

For the fish:
2 lbs. lingcod
1 tbsp. olive oil
1 tbsp. salt
1 tbsp. paprika
1 tbsp. green onion, chopped.
1 tbsp. Italian parsley

DIRECTIONS:

1. For the lemon cream sauce:
2. Chop garlic, shallot, and leeks, then add to a saucepan with oil, salt, pepper, and butter.
3. Sauté over medium heat until the shallot is translucent.
4. Deglaze with white wine, then add whipping cream. Bring the sauce to boil, reduce heat, and simmer for 3 minutes.
5. Remove from heat and add lemon juice and lemon zest. Transfer the sauce to a blender and blend until smooth.
6. Set aside 1/3 cup for the crab mix.
7. For the crab mix:
8. Add all the ingredients to a mixing bowl and mix thoroughly until well combined.
9. Set aside.
10. For the fish:
11. Fire up your Pit boss to high heat, then slice the fish into 6-ounce portions.
12. Lay the fish on its side on a cutting board and slice it ¾ way through the middle leaving a ½-inch on each end to have a nice pouch.
13. Rub the oil into the fish, then place them on a baking sheet. Sprinkle with salt.
14. Stuff crab mix into each fish, then sprinkle paprika and place it on the grill.
15. Cook for 15 minutes or more if the fillets are more than 2-inch thick.
16. Remove the fish and transfer it to a serving platter. Pour the remaining lemon cream sauce on each fish and garnish with onions and parsley.

NUTRITION:

Calories: 476
Total fat: 33 g.

Total carbs: 6 g.
Protein: 38 g.

150. PIT BOSS SMOKED SHRIMP

PREPARATION TIME:	COOKING TIME:	SERVINGS:
10'	10'	6

INGREDIENTS:

1 lb. tail-on shrimp, uncooked
½ tbsp. onion powder
½ tbsp. garlic powder
½ tbsp. salt
4 tbsps. teriyaki sauce
2 tbsps. green onion, minced.
4 tbsps. sriracha mayo

DIRECTIONS:

1. Peel the shrimp shells leaving the tail on, then wash well and rise.
2. Drain well and pat dry with a paper towel. Preheat your Pit boss to 450ºF.
3. Season the shrimp with onion powder, garlic powder, and salt. Place the shrimp in the Pit boss and cook for 6 minutes on each side.
4. Remove the shrimp from the Pit boss and toss with teriyaki sauce, then garnish with onions and mayo.

NUTRITION:

Calories: 87
Total carbs: 2 g.
Protein: 16 g.
Sodium: 1,241 mg.

151. GRILLED SHRIMP KABOBS

PREPARATION TIME:
5'

COOKING TIME:
10'

SERVINGS:
4

INGREDIENTS:

1 lb. colossal shrimp, peeled and deveined.
2 tbsps. oil
½ tbsp. garlic salt
½ tbsp. salt
1/8 tbsp. pepper
6 skewers

DIRECTIONS:

1. Preheat your Pit boss to 375ºF.
2. Pat the shrimp dry with a paper towel.
3. In a mixing bowl, mix oil, garlic salt, salt, and pepper.
4. Toss the shrimp in the mixture until well coated.
5. Skewer the shrimps and cook in the Pit boss with the lid closed for 4 minutes.
6. Open the lid, flip the skewers, cook for another 4 minutes, or wait until the shrimp is pink and the flesh is opaque.
7. Serve.

NUTRITION:

Calories: 325
Protein: 20 g.
Sodium: 120 mg.

152. SWEET BACON-WRAPPED SHRIMP

PREPARATION TIME:
20'

COOKING TIME:
10'

SERVINGS:
12

INGREDIENTS:

1 lb. raw shrimp
½ tbsp. salt
¼ tbsp. garlic powder
1 lb. bacon, cut into halves
Cooking spray

NUTRITION:

Calories: 204
Total fat: 14 g.
Total carbs: 1 g.
Protein: 18 g.

DIRECTIONS:

1. Preheat your Pit boss to 350ºF.
2. Remove the shells and tails from the shrimp, then pat them dry with paper towels.
3. Sprinkle salt and garlic on the shrimp, then wrap with bacon and secure with a toothpick.
4. Place the shrimps on a baking rack greased with cooking spray.
5. Cook for 10 minutes, flip and cook for another 10 minutes, or until the bacon is crisp enough.
6. Remove from the Pit boss and serve.

153. PIT BOSS SPOT PRAWN SKEWERS

PREPARATION TIME:
10'

COOKING TIME:
10'

SERVINGS:
6

INGREDIENTS:

2 lbs. spot prawns
2 tbsps. oil
Salt and pepper to taste

NUTRITION:

Calories: 221
Total fat: 7 g.
Total carbs: 2 g.
Protein: 34 g.

DIRECTIONS:

1. Preheat your Pit boss to 400ºF.
2. Skewer your prawns with soaked skewers, then generously sprinkle with oil, salt, and pepper.
3. Place the skewers on the grill, then cook with the lid closed for 5 minutes on each side.
4. Remove the skewers and serve when hot.

154. PIT BOSS BACON-WRAPPED SCALLOPS

PREPARATION TIME:
15'

COOKING TIME:
20'

SERVINGS:
8

INGREDIENTS:

1 lb. sea scallops
½ lb. bacon

DIRECTIONS:

1. Preheat your Pit boss to 375ºF.
2. Pat dries the scallops with a towel, then wrap them with 1 piece of bacon and secure them with a toothpick.
3. Lay the scallops on the grill with the bacon side down. Close the lid and cook for 5 minutes on each side.
4. Keep the scallops on the bacon side so that you will not get grill marks on the scallops.
5. Serve and enjoy.

NUTRITION:

Calories: 261
Total fat: 14 g.
Total carbs: 5 g.
Protein: 28 g.

155. PIT BOSS LOBSTER TAIL

PREPARATION TIME: 10'	COOKING TIME: 15'	SERVINGS: 2

INGREDIENTS:

10 oz. lobster tail
¼ tbsp. Old Bay seasoning
¼ tbsp. Himalayan salt
2 tbsps. butter, melted.
1 tbsp. fresh parsley, chopped.

DIRECTIONS:

1. Preheat your Pit boss to 450ºF.
2. Slice the tail down the middle, then season it with Old Bay seasoning and salt.
3. Place the tails directly on the grill with the meat side down. Grill for 15 minutes or until the internal temperature reaches 140ºF.
4. Remove from the Pit boss and drizzle with butter.
5. Serve when hot garnished with parsley.

NUTRITION:

Calories: 305
Total fat: 14 g.
Total carbs: 5 g.
Protein: 38 g.

156. GRILLED CAJUN SHRIMP

PREPARATION TIME:
5'

COOKING TIME:
25'

SERVINGS:
8

INGREDIENTS:

For the dip:
½ cup mayonnaise
1 tsp. lemon juice
1 cup sour cream
1 garlic clove, grated.
1 tbsp. Cajun seasoning
1 tbsp. hickory bacon rub
1 tbsp. hot sauce
2 tbsp. Scallions, chopped

For the shrimp:
½ lb. shrimp peeled and deveined.
2 tbsps. olive oil
½ tbsp. hickory bacon seasoning
1 tbsp. Cajun seasoning

DIRECTIONS:

1. Turn on your wood pellet grill.
2. Set it to 350ºF.
3. Mix the dip ingredients in a bowl.
4. Transfer to a small pan.
5. Cover with foil.
6. Place on top of the grill.
7. Cook for 10 minutes.
8. Coat the shrimp with olive oil and sprinkle with the seasonings.
9. Grill for 5 minutes per side.
10. Pour the dip on top or serve with the shrimp.

NUTRITION:
Calories: 87
Total carbs: 2 g.
Net carbs: 2 g.
Protein: 16 g.

157. CAJUN SMOKED SHRIMP

PREPARATION TIME:
10'

COOKING TIME:
10'

SERVINGS:
2

INGREDIENTS:

2 tbsps. extra-virgin olive oil
½ lemon juice
3 garlic cloves, finely minced
2 tbsps. Cajun spice
Salt to taste
1.5 lbs. shrimp, raw, peeled,
deveined.

DIRECTIONS:

1. Take a zip-lock bag and combine olive oil, lemon juice, garlic cloves, Cajun spice, salt, and shrimp. Toss the ingredients well for fine coating.
2. Preheat the smoker grill for 10 minutes until the smoke starts to establish.
3. Put the fish on the grill grate and close the lid.
4. Turn the temperature to high and allow the fish to cook the shrimp for 10 minutes, 5 minutes per side.
5. Once done, serve.

NUTRITION:

Calories: 446
Total Fat: 4.8 g.
Cholesterol: 53 mg.
Sodium: 48 mg.

158. SMOKED CRAB PAPRIKA GARLIC WITH LEMON BUTTER FLAVOR

PREPARATION TIME:	COOKING TIME:	SERVINGS:
5'	30'	10

INGREDIENTS:

7 lbs. (3.2 kg.) fresh crabs

For the sauce:
1 tbsp. salt
1 ½ tsp. cayenne pepper
2 cups salted butter
½ cup lemon juice
1 tbsp. Worcestershire sauce
2 tsps. garlic powder
2 tsps. smoked paprika

DIRECTIONS:

1. Preheat a saucepan over low heat then melt the butter. Let it cool.
2. Season the melted butter, with salt, cayenne pepper, Worcestershire sauce, garlic powder, and smoked paprika, then pour lemon juice into the melted butter. Stir until incorporated and set aside.
3. Then, plug the wood pellet smoker then fill the hopper with the wood pellet. Turn the switch on.
4. Set the wood pellet smoker for indirect heat then adjust the temperature to 350°F (177°C).
5. Arrange the crabs in a disposable aluminum pan; then drizzle the sauce over the crabs.
6. Smoke the crabs for 30 minutes then remove them from the wood pellet smoker.
7. Transfer the smoked crabs to a serving dish then serve.
8. Enjoy!

NUTRITION:
Calories: 455
Fats: 53 g.
Carbs: 3 g.
Fiber: 0 g.

159. CAYENNE GARLIC SMOKED SHRIMP

PREPARATION TIME:	COOKING TIME:	SERVINGS:
5'	*15'*	**10**

INGREDIENTS:

3 lbs. (1.4 kg.) fresh shrimps

For the spices:
2 tbsps. olive oil
2 tbsps. lemon juice
¾ tsp. salt
2 tsps. smoked paprika
½ tsp. pepper
2 tbsps. garlic powder
2 tbsps. onion powder
1 tsp. thyme, dried
2 tsps. cayenne pepper

DIRECTIONS:

1. Combine salt, smoked paprika, pepper, garlic powder, onion powder, dried thyme, and cayenne pepper then mix well. Set aside. Then, peel the shrimps and discard the head. Place in a disposable aluminum pan. Drizzle olive oil and lemon juice over the shrimps and shake to coat. Let the shrimps rest for approximately 5 minutes. Then, plug the wood pellet smoker and fill the hopper with the wood pellet. Turn the switch on.
2. Set the wood pellet smoker for indirect heat; then adjust the temperature to 350°F (177°C).
3. Sprinkle the spice mixture over the shrimps and stir until the shrimps are completely seasoned.
4. Place the disposable aluminum pan with shrimps in the wood pellet smoker and smoke the shrimps for 15 minutes. The shrimps will be opaque and pink. Remove the smoked shrimps from the wood pellet smoker and transfer them to a serving dish.
5. Serve and enjoy.

NUTRITION:
Calories: 233
Fats: 25 g.
Carbs: 7 g.
Fiber: 0 g.

160. CINNAMON GINGER JUICY SMOKED CRAB

PREPARATION TIME: 10'	COOKING TIME: 30'	SERVINGS: 10

INGREDIENTS:

7 lbs. (3.2 kg.) fresh crabs

For the spices:

1 tbsp. salt
3 tbsps. celery seeds, ground
2 tsps. ground mustard
½ tsp. cayenne pepper
½ tsp. black pepper
1 ½ tsp. smoked paprika
A pinch clove, ground
¾ tsp. ground allspice
1 tsp. ginger, ground
½ tsp. cardamom, ground
½ tsp. cinnamon, ground
2 bay leaves

DIRECTIONS:

1. Combine the entire spices—salt, ground celery seeds, mustard, cayenne pepper, black pepper, smoked paprika, clove, allspice, ginger, cardamom, cinnamon, and bay leaves in a bowl. Mix well. Sprinkle the spice mixture over the crabs; then wrap the crabs with aluminum foil. Next, plug the wood pellet smoker and fill the hopper with the wood pellet. Turn the switch on. Set the wood pellet smoker for indirect heat then adjust the temperature to 350°F (177°C). Place the wrapped crabs in the wood pellet smoker and smoke for 30 minutes. Once it is done, remove the wrapped smoked crabs from the wood pellet smoker and let them rest for approximately 10 minutes.
2. Unwrap the smoked crabs and transfer them to a serving dish.
3. Serve and enjoy!

NUTRITION:

Calories: 355
Fats: 22 g.
Carbs: 8 g.
Fiber: 0 g.

161. PARSLEY PRAWN SKEWERS

PREPARATION TIME:	COOKING TIME:	SERVINGS:
15'	8'	5

INGREDIENTS:

¼ cup fresh parsley leaves, minced.
1 tbsp. garlic, crushed.
2½ tbsp. olive oil
2 tbsps. Thai chili sauce
1 tbsp. fresh lime juice
1 ½ lbs. prawns, peeled and deveined.

DIRECTIONS:

1. In a large bowl, add all ingredients except for prawns and mix well.
2. In a resealable plastic bag, add marinade and prawns.
3. Seal the bag and shake to coat well. Refrigerate for about 20–30 minutes.
4. Preheat the Z Grills Pit Boss Grill & Smoker on grill setting to 450ºF.
5. Remove the prawns from the marinade and thread them onto metal skewers.
6. Arrange the skewers onto the grill and cook for about 4 minutes per side.
7. Remove the skewers from the grill and serve hot.

NUTRITION:
Calories: 234
Total fat: 9.3 g.
Total carbs: 4.9 g.
Protein: 31.2 g.

162. BUTTERED SHRIMP

PREPARATION TIME:
15'

COOKING TIME:
30'

SERVINGS:
6

INGREDIENTS:

8 oz. salted butter, melted.
¼ cup Worcestershire sauce
¼ cup fresh parsley, chopped.
1 lemon, quartered.
2 lbs. jumbo shrimp peeled and deveined.
3 tbsps. BBQ rub

DIRECTIONS:

1. In a metal baking pan, add all ingredients except for shrimp and BBQ rub and mix well.
2. Season the shrimp with BBQ rub evenly.
3. Add shrimp in the pan with butter mixture and coat well.
4. Set aside for about 20–30 minutes.
5. Preheat the Z Grills Pit Boss Grill & Smoker on grill setting to 250ºF.
6. Place the pan onto the grill and cook for about 25–30 minutes.
7. Remove the pan from the grill and serve hot.

NUTRITION:

Calories: 462
Fat: 33.3 g.
Total carbs: 4.7 g.
Protein: 34.9 g.

163. PROSCIUTTO WRAPPED SCALLOPS

PREPARATION TIME:
15'

COOKING TIME:
40'

SERVINGS:
4

INGREDIENTS:

8 large scallops shelled and cleaned.
8 slices extra-thin prosciutto

DIRECTIONS:

1. Preheat the Z Grills Pit Boss Grill & Smoker on the grill set to 225–250ºF.
2. Arrange the prosciutto slices onto a smooth surface.
3. Place 1 scallop on the edge of 1 prosciutto slice and roll it up tucking in the sides of the prosciutto to cover completely.
4. Repeat with remaining scallops and prosciutto slices.
5. Arrange the wrapped scallops onto a small wire rack.
6. Place the wire rack onto the grill and cook for about 40 minutes.
7. Remove the scallops from the grill and serve hot.

NUTRITION:

Calories: 160
Fat: 6.7 g.
Total carbs: 1.4 g.
Protein: 23.5 g.

164. BUTTERED CLAMS

PREPARATION TIME:
15'

COOKING TIME:
8'

SERVINGS:
6

INGREDIENTS:

24 littleneck clams
½ cup cold butter, chopped.
2 tbsps. fresh parsley, minced.
3 garlic cloves, minced.
1 tsp. fresh lemon juice

DIRECTIONS:

1. Preheat the Z Grills Pit Boss Grill & Smoker on grill setting to 450ºF.
2. Scrub the clams under cold running water.
3. In a large casserole dish, mix the remaining ingredients.
4. Place the casserole dish onto the grill.
5. Now, arrange the clams directly onto the grill and cook for about 5–8 minutes or until they are opened. (Discard any that fail to open).
6. With tongs, carefully transfer the opened clams into the casserole dish and remove them from the grill.
7. Serve immediately.

NUTRITION:

Calories: 306
Fat: 17.6 g.
Total carbs: 6.4 g.
Protein: 29.3 g.

165. LEMONY LOBSTER TAILS

PREPARATION TIME:	COOKING TIME:	SERVINGS:
15'	25'	4

INGREDIENTS:

½ cup butter, melted.
2 garlic cloves, minced.
2 tsps. fresh lemon juice
Salt and ground black pepper, as required.
4 (8 oz.) lobster tails

DIRECTIONS:

1. Preheat the Z Grills Pit Boss Grill & Smoker on grill setting to 450ºF.
2. In a metal pan, add all ingredients except for lobster tails and mix well.
3. Place the pan onto the grill and cook for about 10 minutes.
4. Meanwhile, cut down the top of the shell and expose lobster meat.
5. Remove the pan of the butter mixture from the grill.
6. Coat the lobster meat with a butter mixture.
7. Place the lobster tails onto the grill and cook for about 15 minutes, coating with butter mixture once halfway through.
8. Remove from the grill and serve hot.

NUTRITION:

Calories: 409
Fat: 24.9 g.
Total carbs: 0.6 g.
Protein: 43.5 g.

11
CHEESE RECIPES

166. SMOKED CHEDDAR CHEESE

PREPARATION TIME:
5'

COOKING TIME:
5 h

SERVINGS:
2

INGREDIENTS:

2 blocks (8 oz.) Cheddar cheese

DIRECTIONS:

1. Preheat and set your Pit Boss grill to 90ºF.
2. Place the cheese blocks directly on the grill grate and smoke for about 4 hours.
3. Remove and transfer into a plastic bag, resealable. Refrigerate for about 2 weeks to allow flavor from smoke to permeate your cheese.
4. Now enjoy!

NUTRITION:

Calories: 115
Total fat: 9.5 g.
Total carbs: 0.9 g.
Protein: 6.5 g.

167. SMOKED MAC AND CHEESE

PREPARATION TIME:	COOKING TIME:	SERVINGS:
2'	1 h	2

INGREDIENTS:

½ cup butter, salted
1/3 cup flour
½ tbsp. salt
6 cups whole milk
Dash Worcestershire sauce
½ tbsp. dry mustard
1 lb. small cooked shells, al dente in well-salted water
2 cups white Cheddar cheese, smoked
2 cups Cheddar jack cheese
1 cup Ritz, crushed

DIRECTIONS:

1. Set your grill on SMOKE and run for about 5–10 minutes with the lid open until fire establishes. Now turn your grill to 325ºF then close the lid.
2. Melt butter in a saucepan, medium, over low--medium heat then whisks in flour.
3. Cook while whisking for about 5–6 minutes over low heat until light tan color.
4. Whisk in salt, milk, Worcestershire, and mustard over low-medium heat stirring frequently until a thickened sauce.
5. Stir small shells, white sauce, and 1 cup cheddar cheese in a large baking dish 10x3-inch high-sided, coated with butter.
6. Top with 1 cup cheddar cheese and Ritz.
7. Place on the grill and bake for about 25–30 minutes until a bubbly mixture and cheese melt.
8. Serve immediately. Enjoy!

NUTRITION:

Calories: 628
Total fat: 42 g.
Total carbs: 38 g.
Protein: 25 g.

168. BERRY COBBLER ON A PIT BOSS GRILL

PREPARATION TIME:	COOKING TIME:	SERVINGS:
15'	35'	8

INGREDIENTS:

For the fruit filling:

3 cups frozen mixed berries
1 tbsp. lemon juice
1 cup brown sugar
1 tbsp. vanilla extract
1 tbsp. lemon zest, finely grated
A pinch salt

For the cobbler topping:

1 ½ cups all-purpose flour
1 ½ tbsp. baking powder
3 tbsps. sugar, granulated
½ tbsp. salt
8 tbsps. cold butter
½ cup sour cream
2 tbsps. raw sugar

DIRECTIONS:

1. Set your Pit Boss grill on SMOKE for about 4–5 minutes with the lid open until fire establishes and your grill starts smoking.
2. Preheat your grill to 350ºF for about 10–15 minutes with the grill lid closed.
3. Meanwhile, combine frozen mixed berries, Lemon juice, brown sugar, vanilla, lemon zest, and a pinch of salt. Transfer into a skillet and let the fruit sit and thaw.
4. Mix flour, baking powder, sugar, and salt in a bowl, medium. Cut cold butter into peas sizes using a pastry blender then add to the mixture. Stir to mix everything.
5. Stir in sour cream until dough starts coming together.
6. Pinch small pieces of dough and place them over the fruit until fully covered. Splash the top with raw sugar.
7. Now place the skillet directly on the grill grate, close the lid, and cook for about 35 minutes until juices bubble, and a golden-brown dough topping.
8. Remove the skillet from the Pit Boss grill and cool for several minutes.
9. Scoop and serve warm.

NUTRITION:

Calories: 371
Total fat: 13 g.
Total carbs: 60 g.
Protein: 3 g.

169. PIT BOSS GRILL APPLE CRISP

PREPARATION TIME:
20'

COOKING TIME:
1 h

SERVINGS:
15

INGREDIENTS:

For the apples:
10 large apples
½ cup flour
1 cup sugar, dark brown
½ tbsp. cinnamon
½ cup butter slices
Cooking spray

For the crisp:
3 cups oatmeal, old-fashioned
1 ½ cups softened butter, salted
1 ½ tbsp. cinnamon
1 cup brown sugar

DIRECTIONS:

1. Preheat your grill to 350ºF.
2. Wash, peel, core, and dice the apples into cubes, medium-size.
3. Mix flour, dark brown sugar, and cinnamon; then toss with your apple cubes.
4. Spray a baking pan, 10x13-inch, with cooking spray then place apples inside. Top with butter slices.
5. Mix all crisp ingredients in a medium bowl until well combined. Place the mixture over the apples.
6. Place on the grill and cook for about 1 hour checking after every 15–20 minutes to ensure cooking is even. Do not place it on the hottest grill part.
7. Remove and let sit for about 20–25 minutes.

NUTRITION:
Calories: 528
Total fat: 26 g.
Total carbs: 75 g.
Protein 4: g.

170. LOW-CARB ALMOND FLOUR BREAD

PREPARATION TIME:	COOKING TIME:	SERVINGS:
10'	1 h 15'	12

INGREDIENTS:

1 tsp. sea salt or to taste
1 tbsp. apple cider vinegar
½ cup warm water
¼ cup coconut oil
4 large eggs, beaten
1 tbsp. gluten-free baking powder
2 cup almond flour, blanched
¼ cup Psyllium husk powder
1 tsp. ginger (optional)

DIRECTIONS:

1. Preheat the grill to 350°F with the lid closed for 15 minutes.
2. Line a 9x5-inch loaf pan with parchment paper. Set aside.
3. Combine the ginger, Psyllium husk powder, almond flour, salt, and baking powder in a large mixing bowl.
4. In another mixing bowl, mix the coconut oil, apple cider vinegar, eggs, and warm water. Mix thoroughly.
5. Gradually pour the flour mixture into the egg mixture, stirring as you pour. Stir until it forms a smooth batter.
6. Fill the lined loaf pan with the batter and cover it with aluminum foil.
7. Place the loaf pan directly on the grill and bake for about 1 hour or until a toothpick or knife inserted in the middle of the bread comes out clean.

NUTRITION:
Calories: 93
Total fat: 7.5 g.
Carbohydrate: 3.6 g.
Protein: 3.1 g.

171. ROSEMARY CHEESE BREAD

PREPARATION TIME:
10'

COOKING TIME:
12'

SERVINGS:
10

INGREDIENTS:

1 ½ cup sunflower seeds
½ tsp. sea salt
1 egg
1 tsp. fresh rosemary, finely chopped
2 tsps. xanthan gum
2 tbsps. cream cheese
2 cups Mozzarella cheese, grated
Cooking spray

DIRECTIONS:

1. Preheat the grill to 400°F with the lid closed for 15 minutes.
2. Toss the sunflower seeds into a powerful blender and blend until it smooth and flour-like.
3. Transfer the sunflower seed flour into a mixing bowl and add the rosemary and xanthan gum. Mix and set aside.
4. Melt the Mozzarella cheese in a microwave. To do this, combine the cream cheese and mozzarella cheese in a microwave-safe dish.
5. Place the microwave-safe dish in the grill and heat the cheese on HIGH for 1 minute.
6. Bring out the dish and stir. Place the dish in the grill and heat for 30 seconds. Bring out the dish and stir until smooth.
7. Pour the melted cheese into a large mixing bowl.
8. Add the sunflower flour mixture to the melted cheese and stir the ingredients are well combined.
9. Add the salt and egg and mix thoroughly to form a smooth dough.
10. Measure out equal pieces of the dough and roll them into sticks.
11. Grease a baking sheet with oil and arrange the breadsticks into the baking sheet in a single layer.
12. Use the back of a knife or metal spoon to make lines on the breadsticks.
13. Place the baking sheet on the grill and make for about 12 minutes or until the breadsticks turn golden brown.
14. Remove the baking sheet from the grill and let the breadsticks cool for a few minutes.
15. Serve.

NUTRITION:
Calories: 23
Total fat: 1.9 g.
Total carbohydrate: 0.6 g.
Protein: 1.2 g.

172. CINNAMON ALMOND SHORTBREAD

PREPARATION TIME:
20'

COOKING TIME:
20'

SERVINGS:
5

INGREDIENTS:

2 tsps. cinnamon
½ cup unsalted butter, softened
1 large egg, beaten
½ tsp. salt or to taste
2 cups almond flour
¼ cup sugar
1 tsp. ginger (optional)

DIRECTIONS:

1. Preheat the grill to 300°F with the lid closed for 5 minutes.
2. Grease a cookie sheet with oil.
3. In a large bowl, combine the cinnamon, almond flour, sugar, ginger, and salt. Mix thoroughly to combine.
4. In another mixing bowl, whisk the egg and softened butter together.
5. Pour the egg mixture into the flour mixture and combine until a smooth batter forms.
6. Use a tbsp. to measure out equal amounts of the mixture and roll into balls.
7. Arrange the balls into the cookie sheet in a single layer.
8. Now, use the flat bottom of a clean glass cup to press each ball into a flat round cookie. Grease the bottom of the cup before using it to press the balls.
9. Place the cookie sheet on the grill and bake until browned. This will take about 20–25 minutes.
10. Remove the cookie sheet from the grill and let the shortbreads cool for a few minutes.
11. Serve and enjoy.

NUTRITION:

Calories: 152
Total fat: 12.7 g.
Total carbs: 6.5 g.
Protein: 3.5 g.

173. SIMPLE ROASTED BUTTERNUT SQUASH

PREPARATION TIME:
5'

COOKING TIME:
25'

SERVINGS:
8

INGREDIENTS:

1 (2 lbs.) butternut squash
2 garlic cloves, minced
2 tbsps. extra olive virgin oil
1 tsp. paprika
1 tsp. oregano
1 tsp. thyme
Salt and pepper to taste

DIRECTIONS:

1. Start your grill on SMOKE mode and leave it open for 5 minutes, until the fire preheats the grill to 400°F.
2. Peel the butternut squash.
3. Cut the butternut squash into 2 (cut lengthwise).
4. Use a spoon to scoop out the seeds.
5. Cut the butternut squash into 1-inch chunks and wash the chunks with water.
6. In a big bowl, combine the butternut squash chunks and other ingredients.
7. Stir until the chunks are coated with the ingredients.
8. Spread the coated chunks on the sheet pan.
9. Place the sheet pan on the grill and bake for 25 minutes.
10. Remove the baked butternut squash from heat and let it sit to cool.
11. Serve.

NUTRITION:

Calories: 8
Total fat: 3.7 g.
Carbohydrates: 13.8 g.
Protein: 1.2 g.

174. MANGO BREAD

PREPARATION TIME:
15'

COOKING TIME:
1 h

SERVINGS:
4

INGREDIENTS:

2 ½ cup ripe mangoes, cubed
2 cups all-purpose flour
1 tsp. baking powder
1 tsp. baking soda
2 eggs, beaten
1 tsp. cinnamon
1 tsp. vanilla extract
½ tsp. nutmeg
¾ cup olive oil
¾ cup sugar
1 tbsp. lemon juice
½ tsp. salt
½ cup dates, chopped

DIRECTIONS:

1. Start your grill on smoke MODE and leave the lid opened for 5 minutes, or until the fire starts.
2. Close the lid and preheat the grill to 350°F for 15 minutes, using alder hard Pit Boss.
3. Grease an 8x4-inch loaf pan.
4. In a mixing bowl, combine the flour, baking powder, baking soda, cinnamon, salt, and sugar.
5. In another mixing bowl, whisk together the egg, lemon juice, oil, and vanilla.
6. Pour the egg mixture into the flour mixture and mix until you well combined.
7. Fold in the mangoes and dates.
8. Pour the mixture into the loaf pan and place the pan on the grill.
9. Place the loaf pan directly on the grill bake for about 50–60 minutes or until a toothpick inserted in the middle of the bread comes out clean.
10. After the baking cycle, remove the loaf pan from the grill and transfer the bread to a wire rack to cool completely.
11. Slice and serve.

NUTRITION:
Calories: 856
Total fat: 41.2 g.
Carbohydrates: 118.9 g.
Protein: 10.7 g.

175. BAKED S'MORES DONUT

PREPARATION TIME:
10'

COOKING TIME:
35'

SERVINGS:
8-12

INGREDIENTS:

For the donuts:
1 cup all-purpose flour
Cooking spray
¼ tsp. baking soda
1/3 cup sugar
¾ cup buttermilk
2 tbsps. butter, unsalted
1 egg
½ tsp. vanilla extract
4 chocolate bars (whatever kind you want)
24 marshmallows, sliced in half

For the glaze:
¼ cup whole milk
1 tsp. vanilla extract
2 cups confectioner's sugar

NUTRITION:
Calories: 217
Fat: 5 g.
Carbohydrates: 32 g.
Protein: 11 g.

DIRECTIONS:

Grill Prep:
1. Spray the donut pans with some cooking spray.
2. Mix sugar, flour, and baking soda.
3. Grab a different bowl; whisk your egg, melted butter, buttermilk, and vanilla.
4. Mix the dry and wet ingredients using a spatula, blending them perfectly.
5. Pipe your batter onto your greased donut pans.

On the grill:
6. Set up your wood pellet smoker grill for indirect cooking.
7. Preheat your wood pellet smoker grill for 10–15 minutes at 350°F.
8. Bake your batter for 25 minutes, till your donuts are nice and puffy, and the toothpick you insert to check it comes out nice and clean. Then let it cool in the pan.
9. Mix your vanilla and milk in a saucepan and heat it over low heat till it's a bit warm.
10. Sift your confectioner's sugar into your milk and vanilla mix till it's wonderfully combined.
11. Take your glaze off the fire, and let it set on a bowl of warm water.
12. Take your delicious donuts and dip them right into your glaze, then set your cooling rack over some foil, and then put your donuts on the shelf, letting them rest for 5 minutes.
13. Halve your donuts, and then place your halved marshmallows in between, as well as some chocolate.
14. Grill these sandwiches for 4–5 minutes. You want the chocolate and marshmallows to melt.
15. Take them off the grill, serve, and enjoy!

176. BAKED CHERRY CHEESECAKE GALETTE

PREPARATION TIME:	COOKING TIME:	SERVINGS:
10'	20'	6-8

INGREDIENTS:

For the cherry filling:
1 lb. cherries, thawed, drained
¼ cup sugar
1 tsp. cornstarch
1 tsp. coriander
A pinch salt
1 tbsp. orange zest
½ tbsp. lemon zest

For the cream cheese filling:
8 oz. cream cheese, softened
1 tsp. vanilla
¼ cup sugar
1 egg

For the galette:
1 pie crust, refrigerated
1 egg
1 tbsp. water, cream, or milk
1 tbsp. Sugar, granulated
Vanilla ice cream to serve

DIRECTIONS:

1. Grab a medium bowl; mix your cherries, orange zest, lemon zest, and coriander, half of the sugar, cornstarch, and a pinch of salt.
2. Grab another bowl, and in it, mix your egg, vanilla, sugar, and cream cheese. Whip it up.
3. Get your pie dough onto a sheet tray, and then stretch it out with a rolling pin. Get it to about 1-inch in diameter.
4. Spread out your cream cheese filling in the middle of the pie dough. Be careful to leave a border of 1-inch around the edge. Then pile your cherry mix on the cream cheese.
5. Now, you are going to fold the edges of the pie crust into small pieces over the filling.
6. Next, brush the edges of the pie dough with egg wash, and then sprinkle on some granulated sugar.

On the grill:

1. Set up your wood pellet smoker grill for indirect cooking.
2. Preheat your wood pellet smoker grill at a temperature of 350°F, keeping it closed for 15 minutes.
3. Set your sheet to try right on the grill grate, and then bake that yummy goodness for 15–20 minutes. You want the crust to become nice and golden brown and for the cheesecake filling to be completely set.
4. Dish the galette while warm with some ice cream. And then enjoy.

NUTRITION:
Calories: 400
Fat: 51 g.
Carbohydrates: 18 g.
Protein: 5 g.

177. SMOKED SALTED CARAMEL APPLE PIE

PREPARATION TIME:	COOKING TIME:	SERVINGS:
30'	30'	4-6

INGREDIENTS:

For the apple pie:
1 pastry (for double-crust pie)
6 Apples

For the smoked, salted caramel:
1 cup brown sugar
¾ cup light corn syrup
6 tbsps. unsalted butter, cut into pieces
1 cup warm smoked cream
1 tsp. sea salt
1 cup raw sugar

DIRECTIONS:

For the grill prep:
1. Fill a container with water and ice.
2. Grab a shallow, smaller pan, and then put in your cream. Take that smaller pan and place it in the large pan with ice and water.
3. Set this on your wood pellet smoker grill for 15–20 minutes.
4. For the caramel, mix your corn syrup and sugar in a saucepan, and then cook it all using medium heat. Be sure to stir every so often until the back of your spoon is coated and begins to turn copper.
5. Next, add the butter, salt, and smoked cream, and then stir.
6. Get your pie crust, apples, and salted caramel. Put a pie crust on a pie plate, and then fill it with slices of apples.
7. Pour on the caramel next.
8. Put on the top crust over all of that, and then crimp both crusts together to keep them locked in.
9. Create a few slits in the top crust so that the steam can be released as you bake.
10. Brush with some cream or egg, and then sprinkle with some sea salt and raw sugar.

For cooking on the grill:
11. Set up your wood pellet smoker grill for indirect cooking.
12. Preheat your wood pellet smoker grill for 10–15 minutes at 375ºF, keeping the lid closed as soon as the fire gets started (should take 4–5 minutes, tops).
13. Set the pie on your grill, and then bake for 20 minutes.
14. At the 20 minutes mark, lower the heat to 325ºF, and then let it cook for 35 minutes more. You want the crust to be a nice golden brown, and the filling should be bubbly when it's ready.
15. Take the pie off the grill and allow it to cool and rest.
16. Serve with some vanilla ice cream and enjoy!

NUTRITION:
Calories: 149
Fat: 2 g.
Carbohydrates: 30 g.
Protein: 3 g.

178. PIT BOSS GRILL FLATBREAD PIZZA

PREPARATION TIME:	COOKING TIME:	SERVINGS:
10'	20'	3

INGREDIENTS:

For the dough:
2 cups flour
1 tbsp. salt
1 tbsp. sugar
2 tbsps. yeast
6 oz. warm water

For the toppings:
1 green/red bell pepper
½ garlic
1 zucchini
½ onion
½ tsp. olive oil
5 strips bacon
1 cup yellow cherry tomatoes, halved
2 jalapeños, sliced
2 green olives, sliced
2 kalamata olives, sliced
1 tbsp. goat cheese

For drizzling:
Balsamic vinegar

DIRECTIONS:

1. Combine all dough ingredients in a stand mixer bowl. Mix until the dough is smooth and elastic. Divide into 3 equal balls.
2. Roll each dough ball with a rolling pin into a thin round enough to fit a 12-inch skillet.
3. Grease the skillet using olive oil.
4. Meanwhile, turn your Pit Boss Grill on SMOKE for about 4–5 minutes with the lid open. Turn to high and preheat for about 10–15 minutes with the lid closed.
5. Once ready, arrange peppers, garlic, zucchini, and onion on the grill grate then drizzle with oil and salt. Check at 10 minutes.
6. Now remove zucchini from the grill and add bacon. Continue to cook for another 10 minutes until bacon is done.
7. Transfer the toppings on a chopping board to cool. Chop tomatoes, jalapeños, and olives.
8. Brush your crust with oil and smash garlic with a fork over the crust. Smear carefully not to tear the crust.
9. Add toppings to the crust in the skillet.
10. Place the skillet on the grill and cook for about 20 minutes until brown edges.
11. Repeat for the other crusts.
12. Now drizzle each with vinegar and slice.
13. Serve and enjoy.

NUTRITION:
Calories: 342
Total fat: 1.2 g.
Total carbs: 70.7 g.
Protein: 11.7 g.

179. PIT BOSS SMOKED NUT MIX

PREPARATION TIME:	COOKING TIME:	SERVINGS:
15'	20'	8

INGREDIENTS:

3 cups mixed nuts (pecans, peanuts, almonds, etc.)
½ tbsp. brown sugar
1 tbsp. thyme, dried
¼ tbsp. mustard powder
1 tbsp. extra-virgin olive oil

DIRECTIONS:

1. Preheat your Pit Boss Grill to 250ºF with the lid closed for about 15 minutes.
2. Combine all ingredients in a large bowl, then transfer them into a cookie sheet lined with parchment paper.
3. Place the cookie sheet on a grill and grill for about 20 minutes.
4. Remove the nuts from the grill and let them cool.
5. Serve and enjoy.

NUTRITION:

Calories: 249
Total fat: 21.5 g.
Total carbs: 12.3 g.
Protein: 5.7 g.

180. PIT BOSS GRILL CHICKEN FLATBREAD

PREPARATION TIME:	COOKING TIME:	SERVINGS:
5'	30'	6

INGREDIENTS:

6 mini pieces of bread
1 ½ cups buffalo sauce, divided
4 cups chicken breasts, cooked and cubed

For drizzling
Mozzarella cheese

DIRECTIONS:

1. Preheat your Pit Boss Grill to 375–400ºF.
2. Place the bread on a flat surface, then evenly spread ½ cup buffalo sauce on all bread.
3. Toss together chicken breasts and 1 cup buffalo sauce then top over all the bread evenly.
4. Top each with mozzarella cheese.
5. Place the bread directly on the grill but over indirect heat. Close the lid.
6. Cook for about 5–7 minutes until slightly toasty edges, cheese is melted, and fully hated chicken.
7. Remove and drizzle with ranch or blue cheese.
8. Enjoy!

NUTRITION:
Calories: 346
Total fat: 7.6 g.
Total carbs: 33.9 g.
Protein: 32.5 g.

181. GRILLED HOMEMADE CROUTON

PREPARATION TIME:	COOKING TIME:	SERVINGS:
10'	30'	6

INGREDIENTS:

2 tbsps. Mediterranean Blend Seasoning
¼ cup olive oil
6 cups bread, cubed

DIRECTIONS:

1. Preheat your Pit Boss Grill to 250ºF.
2. Combine seasoning and oil in a bowl then drizzle the mixture over the bread cubes. Toss to evenly coat.
3. Layer the bread cubes on a cookie sheet, large, and place them on the grill.
4. Bake for about 30 minutes. Stir at intervals of 5 minutes for browning evenly.
5. Once dried out and golden brown, remove it from the grill.
6. Serve and enjoy!

NUTRITION:

Calories: 188
Total fat: 10 g.
Total carbs: 20 g.
Protein: 4 g.

12
VEGETABLES RECIPES

182. WOOD PELLET BACON WRAPPED JALAPEÑO POPPERS

PREPARATION TIME:
10'

COOKING TIME:
20'

SERVINGS:
6

INGREDIENTS:

6 fresh jalapeños
4 oz. cream cheese
½ cup Cheddar cheese, shredded
1 tbsp. vegetable rub
12 slices cut bacon

DIRECTIONS:

1. Preheat the wood pellet smoker and grill to 375°F.
2. Slice the jalapeños lengthwise and scrape the seed and membrane. Rinse them with water and set them aside.
3. Mix cream cheese, cheddar cheese, and vegetable rub until well mixed.
4. Fill the jalapeño halves with the mixture, then wrap them with the bacon pieces.
5. Smoke for 20 minutes or until the bacon crispy.
6. Serve and enjoy.

NUTRITION:

Calories: 1830
Total fat: 11 g.
Total carbs: 5 g.
Protein: 6 g.

183. WOOD-PELLET-GRILLED MEXICAN STREET CORN

PREPARATION TIME:
5'

COOKING TIME:
25'

SERVINGS:
6

INGREDIENTS:

6 ears corn on the cob, shucked
1 tbsp. olive oil
Kosher salt and pepper to taste
¼ cup mayo
¼ cup sour cream
1 tbsp. garlic paste
½ tbsp. chili powder
A pinch of ground red pepper
½ cup cotija cheese, crumbled
¼ cup cilantro, chopped
6 lime wedges

DIRECTIONS:

1. Brush the corn with oil and dash with salt and pepper.
2. Place the corn on a wood pellet grill set at 350°F. Cook for 25 minutes as you turn it occasionally.
3. Meanwhile, mix mayo, cream cheese, garlic, chili, and red pepper until well combined.
4. When the corn is cooked, remove it from the grill, rest for some minutes, and brush with the mayo mixture.
5. Sprinkle cotija cheese, more chili powder, and cilantro. Serve with lime wedges. Enjoy.

NUTRITION:

Calories: 144
Total fat: 5 g.
Total carbs: 10 g.
Potassium: 173 mg.

184. WOOD-PELLET-GRILLED STUFFED ZUCCHINI

PREPARATION TIME:
5'

COOKING TIME:
11'

SERVINGS:
8

INGREDIENTS:

4 zucchinis
5 tbsps. olive oil
2 tbsps. red onion, chopped
¼ tbsp. garlic, minced
½ cup breadcrumbs
½ cup Mozzarella cheese, shredded
1 tbsp. fresh mint
½ tbsp. salt
3 tbsps. Parmesan cheese

DIRECTIONS:

1. Slice the zucchini lengthwise and scoop out the pulp, then brush the shells with oil.
2. In a non-stick skillet, sauté the pulp, onion, and remaining oil. Add garlic and cook for 1 minute.
3. Add breadcrumbs and cook until golden brown. Remove from heat and stir in Mozzarella cheese, fresh mint, and salt.
4. Spoon the mixture into the shells and dash Parmesan cheese.
5. Place in a grill and grill for 10 minutes or until the zucchini is tender.

NUTRITION:

Calories: 186
Total fat: 10 g.
Total carbs: 17 g.
Protein: 9 g.

'185. WOOD-PELLET-GRILLED SPICY SWEET POTATOES

PREPARATION TIME:	COOKING TIME:	SERVINGS:
10'	35'	6

INGREDIENTS:

2 lbs. sweet potatoes, cut into chunks
1 red onion, chopped
2 tbsps. oil
2 tbsps. orange juice
1 tbsp. cinnamon, roasted
1 tbsp. salt
¼ tbsp. Chipotle chili pepper

DIRECTIONS:

1. Preheat the wood pellet grill to 425°F with the lid closed.
2. Toss the sweet potatoes with onion, oil, and orange juice.
3. In a mixing bowl, mix cinnamon, salt, and chili pepper, then sprinkle the mixture over the sweet potatoes. Spread the potatoes on a lined baking dish in a single layer.
4. Place the baking dish in the grill and grill for 30 minutes or until the sweet potatoes are tender.
5. Serve and enjoy.

NUTRITION:

Calories: 145
Total fat: 5 g.
Total carbs: 23 g.
Protein: 2 g.

186. WOOD-PELLET-SMOKED VEGETABLES

PREPARATION TIME:	COOKING TIME:	SERVINGS:
5'	15'	6

INGREDIENTS:

1 ear corn, fresh, husks and silk strands removed
1 yellow squash, sliced
1 red onion, cut into wedges
1 green pepper, cut into strips
1 red pepper, cut into strips
1 yellow pepper, cut into strips
1 cup mushrooms, halved
2 tbsps. oil
2 tbsps. chicken seasoning

DIRECTIONS:

1. Soak the pecan wood pellets in water for 1 hour. Remove the pellets from the water and fill the smoker box with the wet pellets.
2. Place the smoker box under the grill and close the lid. Heat the grill on high for 10 minutes or until smoke starts coming out from the wood chips.
3. Meanwhile, toss the veggies in oil and seasonings, then transfer them into a grill basket.
4. Grill for 10 minutes while turning occasionally. Serve and enjoy.

NUTRITION:

Calories: 97
Total fat: 5 g.
Total carbs: 11 g.
Protein: 2 g.

187. VEGAN SMOKED CARROT DOGS

PREPARATION TIME:
25'

COOKING TIME:
35'

SERVINGS:
4

INGREDIENTS:

4 thick carrots
2 tbsps. avocado oil
1 tbsp. liquid smoke
½ tbsp. garlic powder
Salt and pepper to taste

DIRECTIONS:

1. Preheat the wood pellet grill to 425°F and line a baking sheet with parchment paper.
2. Peel the carrots and round the edges.
3. In a mixing bowl, mix oil, liquid smoke, garlic, salt, and pepper. Place the carrots on the baking dish, then pour the mixture over.
4. Roll the carrots to coat evenly with the mixture and use fingertips to massage the mixture into the carrots. Place in the grill and grill for 35 minutes or until the carrots are fork-tender, ensuring to turn and brush the carrots every 5 minutes with the marinade.
5. Remove from the grill and place the carrots in a hot dog bun. Serve with your favorite toppings and enjoy.

NUTRITION:

Calories: 149
Total fat: 1.6 g.
Total carbs: 27.9 g.
Protein: 5.4 g.

188. WOOD-PELLET-SMOKED ASPARAGUS

PREPARATION TIME:
5'

COOKING TIME:
60'

SERVINGS:
4

INGREDIENTS:

1 bunch fresh asparagus ends cut
2 tbsps. olive oil
Salt and pepper to taste

DIRECTIONS:

1. Fire up your wood pellet smoker to 230°F.
2. Lay the asparagus in a mixing bowl and drizzle with olive oil. Season with salt and pepper.
3. Place the asparagus on a sheet of aluminum foil and fold the sides such that you create a basket.
4. Smoke the asparagus for 1 hour or until soft turning after ½ hour.
5. Remove from the grill and serve. Enjoy.

NUTRITION:

Calories: 43
Total fat: 2 g.
Total carbs: 4 g.
Protein: 3 g.

189. SMOKED DEVILED EGGS

PREPARATION TIME:	COOKING TIME:	SERVINGS:
15'	30'	5

INGREDIENTS:

7 eggs, hard-boiled, peeled
3 tbsps. mayonnaise
3 tbsps. chives, diced
1 tbsp. brown mustard
1 tbsp. apple cider vinegar
Dash hot sauce
Salt and pepper to taste
2 tbsps. cooked bacon, crumbled
Paprika to taste

DIRECTIONS:

1. Preheat the wood pellet to 180°F for 15 minutes with the lid closed.
2. Place the eggs on the grill grate and smoke the eggs for 30 minutes. Remove the eggs from the grill and let cool.
3. Half the eggs and scoop the egg yolks into a zip-lock bag.
4. Add all other ingredients in the zip-lock bag except bacon and paprika. Mix until smooth.
5. Pipe the mixture into the egg whites, then top with bacon and paprika.
6. Let rest, then serve and enjoy.

NUTRITION:

Calories: 140
Total fat: 12 g.
Total carbs: 1 g.
Protein 6 g.

190. WHOLE-ROASTED CAULIFLOWER WITH GARLIC PARMESAN BUTTER

PREPARATION TIME:	COOKING TIME:	SERVINGS:
15'	45'	5

INGREDIENTS:

¼ cup olive oil
Salt and pepper to taste
1 fresh cauliflower
½ cup butter, melted
¼ cup Parmesan cheese, grated
1 garlic clove, minced
½ tbsp. parsley, chopped

DIRECTIONS:

1. Preheat the wood pellet grill with the lid closed for 15 minutes.
2. Meanwhile, brush the cauliflower with oil, then season with salt and pepper.
3. Place the cauliflower in a cast iron and place it on a grill grate.
4. Cook for 45 minutes or until the cauliflower is golden brown and tender.
5. Meanwhile, mix butter, Parmesan cheese, garlic, and parsley in a mixing bowl.
6. In the last 20 minutes of cooking, add the butter mixture.
7. Remove the cauliflower from the grill and top with more cheese and parsley if you desire.
8. Enjoy.

NUTRITION:

Calories 156
Total fat: 11.1 g.
Total carbs: 8.8 g.
Protein: 8.2 g.

191. MEXICAN STREET CORN WITH CHIPOTLE BUTTER

PREPARATION TIME:
10'

COOKING TIME:
14'

SERVINGS:
4

INGREDIENTS:

4 ears corn
½ cup sour cream
½ cup mayonnaise
¼ cup fresh cilantro, chopped
Chipotle butter, for topping
1 cup Parmesan cheese, grated

DIRECTIONS:

1. Supply your smoker with wood pellets and follow the manufacturer's specific start-up procedure.
2. Preheat with the lid closed to 450°F.
3. Shuck the corn, removing the silks, and cutting off the cores.
4. Tear 4 squares of aluminum foil large enough to cover an ear of corn completely.
5. In a medium bowl, combine the sour cream, mayonnaise, and cilantro. Slather the mixture all over the ears of corn.
6. Wrap each ear of corn in a piece of foil, sealing tightly. Place on the grill, close the lid and smoke for 12–14 minutes.
7. Get rid of the corn from the foil and place it in a shallow baking dish. Top with chipotle butter, Parmesan cheese, and more chopped cilantro.
8. Serve immediately.

NUTRITION:

Calories: 150
Carbohydrates: 15 g.
Protein: 79 g.
Sodium: 45 mg.

192. TWICE-SMOKED POTATOES

PREPARATION TIME:	COOKING TIME:	SERVINGS:
10'	14'	4

INGREDIENTS:

8 Idaho, Russet, or Yukon Gold potatoes
1 cup Parmesan cheese, grated
½ lb. bacon, cooked and crumbled
¼ cup scallions, chopped
Salt and freshly ground black pepper to taste
1 cup Cheddar cheese, shredded

DIRECTIONS:

1. Supply your smoker with wood pellets and follow the manufacturer's specific start-up procedure.
2. Preheat with the lid closed to 400°F.
3. Poke the potatoes all over with a fork. Arrange them directly on the grill grate, close the lid, and smoke for 1 hour and 15 minutes, or until cooked through, and they have some give when pinched.
4. Let the potatoes cool for 10 minutes, then cut in half lengthwise.
5. Into a medium bowl, scoop out the potato flesh, leaving ¼-inch in the shells, place the shells on a baking sheet.
6. Stir in the Parmesan cheese, bacon, and scallions, and season with salt and pepper.
7. Generously stuff each shell with the potato mixture and top with Cheddar cheese.
8. Set the baking sheet on the grill grate, close the lid, and smoke for 20 minutes, or until the cheese is melted.

NUTRITION:

Calories: 150
Carbohydrates: 15 g.
Protein: 79 g.
Sodium: 45 mg.

193. ROASTED OKRA

PREPARATION TIME:
10'

COOKING TIME:
30'

SERVINGS:
4

INGREDIENTS:

1 lb. whole okra
2 tbsps. extra-virgin olive oil
2 tsps. seasoned salt
2 tsps. freshly ground black pepper
Cooking spray

DIRECTIONS:

1. Supply your smoker with wood pellets and follow the manufacturer's specific start-up procedure.
2. Preheat with the lid closed to 400°F. Alternatively, preheat your oven to 400°F.
3. Line a shallow rimmed baking pan with aluminum foil and coat with cooking spray.
4. Arrange the okra on the pan in a single layer. Drizzle with the olive oil, turning to coat—season on all sides with salt and pepper.
5. Place the baking pan on the grill grate, close the lid, and smoke for 30 minutes, or until crisp and slightly charred. Alternatively, roast it in the oven for 30 minutes.
6. Serve hot.

NUTRITION:

Calories: 150
Carbohydrates: 15 g.
Protein: 79 g.
Sodium: 45 mg.

194. MUSHROOMS STUFFED WITH CRAB MEAT

PREPARATION TIME:
20'

COOKING TIME:
45'

SERVINGS:
6

INGREDIENTS:

6 medium Portobello mushrooms
Extra-virgin olive oil
1/3 cup parmesan cheese, grated

For the crab meat stuffing:

8 oz. fresh crab meat canned or imitation crab meat
2 tbsps. extra-virgin olive oil
1/3 celery, chopped
red peppers, chopped
½ cup green onion, chopped
½ cup Italian breadcrumbs

DIRECTIONS:

1. Clean up the mushroom cap with a damp paper towel. Cut off the stem and save it.
2. Remove the brown gills from the bottom of the mushroom cap with a spoon and discard.
3. Prepare crab meat stuffing. If you are a fan of using canned crab meat, drain, rinse, and remove shellfish.
4. Put the crab mixture in each mushroom cap and make a mound in the center.
5. Sprinkle extra-virgin olive oil and sprinkle parmesan cheese on each stuffed mushroom cap. Put the mushrooms in a 10x15-inch baking dish.
6. Use the pellets to set the wood pellet smoker and grill to indirect heating and preheat to 375°F.
7. Bake for 30–45 minutes until the filling becomes hot (165ºF as measured by an instant-read digital thermometer), and the mushrooms begin to release juice.

NUTRITION:

Calories: 160
Carbs: 14 g.
Fat: 8 g.
Protein: 10 g.

195. BRISKET BAKED BEANS

PREPARATION TIME:
20'

COOKING TIME:
2 h

SERVINGS:
10

INGREDIENTS:

2 tbsps. extra-virgin olive oil
1 large onion, diced
1 green pepper, diced
1 red pepper diced
2–6 jalapeño peppers diced
3 Texas-style brisket flat, chopped
1 baked bean, like Bush's country-
style baked beans
1 can pork and beans
1 red kidney beans, rinse, drain
1 cup barbecue sauce like Sweet
Baby Ray's®
½ cup brown sugar, stuffed
3 garlic, chopped
2 tsps. mustard
½ tsp. kosher salt
½ tsp. black pepper

DIRECTIONS:

1. Heat the skillet with olive oil over medium heat and add the diced onion, peppers, and jalapeño. Sauté for about 8–10 minutes until the onion is translucent.
2. In a 4-quart casserole dish, mix chopped brisket, baked beans, pork beans, kidney beans, cooked onions, peppers, barbecue sauce, brown sugar, garlic, mustard, salt, and black pepper.
3. Using the selected pellets, configure the wood pellet smoking grill for indirect cooking and preheat to 325°F.
4. Cook the beans baked in the brisket for 1.5–2 hours until they become raw beans.
5. Rest for 15 minutes before eating.

NUTRITION:
Calories: 199
Carbs: 35 g.
Fat: 2 g.
Protein: 9 g.

196. APPLE-WOOD-SMOKED CHEESE

PREPARATION TIME:
1 h 15'

COOKING TIME:
2 h

SERVINGS:
6

INGREDIENTS:

Gouda
Sharp cheddar
Very sharp 3-year cheddar
Monterey Jack
Pepper jack
Swiss

DIRECTIONS:

1. According to the cheese block's shape, cut the cheese block into an easy-to-handle size (approximately 4x4-inch block) to promote smoke penetration.
2. Leave the cheese on the counter for 1 hour to form a very thin skin or crust, which acts as a heat barrier but allows smoke to penetrate.
3. Configure the wood pellet smoking grill for indirect heating and install a cold smokebox to prepare for cold smoke. Ensure that the louvers on the smoking box are fully open to allow moisture to escape from the box.
4. Preheat the wood pellet smoker and grill to 180°F or use apple pellets and smoke settings, if any, to get a milder smoke flavor.
5. Place the cheese on a Teflon-coated fiberglass non-stick grill mat and let cool for 2 hours.
6. Remove the smoked cheese and cool for 1 hour on the counter using a cooling rack.
7. After labeling the smoked cheese with a vacuum seal, refrigerate for 2 weeks or more, then smoke will permeate, and the cheese flavor will become milder.

NUTRITION:

Calories: 102
Carbs: 0 g.
Fat: 9
Protein: 6 g.

197. ATOMIC BUFFALO TURDS

PREPARATION TIME:	COOKING TIME:	SERVINGS:
45	2 h	6

INGREDIENTS:

10 medium jalapeño pepper
8 oz. regular cream cheese at room temperature
¾ cup Monterey Jack and Cheddar Cheese Blend Shred (optional)
1 tsp. smoked paprika
1 tsp. garlic powder
½ tsp. cayenne pepper
Tsp. red pepper flakes (optional)
20 smoky sausages
10 slices bacon, cut in half

DIRECTIONS:

1. Wear food service gloves when using them. Jalapeño peppers are washed vertically and sliced. Carefully remove seeds and veins using a spoon or paring knife and discard. Place jalapeño on a grilled vegetable tray and set aside.
2. In a small bowl, mix cream cheese, shredded cheese, paprika, garlic powder, cayenne pepper is used, and red pepper flakes if used, until thoroughly mixed.
3. Mix cream cheese with half of the jalapeño pepper.
4. Place the little smokiness sausages on half of the filled jalapeño pepper.
5. Wrap half of the thin bacon around half of each jalapeño pepper.
6. Fix the bacon to the sausage with a toothpick so that the pepper does not pierce. Place the ABT on the grill tray or pan.
7. Set the wood pellet smoker and grill for indirect cooking and preheat to 250ºF using hickory pellets or blends.
8. Suck jalapeño peppers at 250°F for about 1.5−2 hours until the bacon is cooked and crisp.
9. Remove the ABT from the grill and let it rest for 5 minutes.

NUTRITION:

Calories: 131
Carbs: 1 g.
Fat: 12 g.
Protein: 5 g.

198. SMOKED GUACAMOLE

PREPARATION TIME:
15'

COOKING TIME:
30'

SERVINGS:
8

INGREDIENTS:

¼ cup cilantro, chopped
7 avocados, peeled and seeded
¼ cup red onion, chopped
¼ cup tomato, chopped
3 ears corn
1 tsp. chili powder
1 tsp. cumin
2 tbsps. lime juice
1 tbsp. garlic, minced
1 chili poblano
Black pepper and salt to taste

DIRECTIONS:

1. Preheat the grill to 180ºF with a closed lid.
2. Smoke the avocado for 10 minutes.
3. Set the avocados aside and increase the temperature of the girl to high.
4. Once heated, grill the corn and chili—roast for 20 minutes.
5. Cut the corn. Set aside. Place the chili in a bowl. Cover it with a wrapper and let it sit for about 10 minutes. Peel the chili and dice. Add it to the kernels.
6. In a bowl, mash the avocados, leave few chunks. Add the remaining ingredients and mix.
7. Serve right away because it is best eaten fresh. Enjoy!

NUTRITION:

Calories: 51
Protein: 1 g.
Carbs: 3 g.
Fat: 4.5 g.

199. ROASTED CASHEWS

PREPARATION TIME:
15'

COOKING TIME:
12'

SERVINGS:
6

INGREDIENTS:

¼ cup rosemary, chopped
2 ½ tbsp. butter, melted
2 cups cashews, raw
½ tsp. cayenne pepper
1 tsp. salt

DIRECTIONS:

1. Preheat the grill to 350ºF with a closed lid.
2. In a baking dish, layer the nuts. Combine the cayenne, salt, rosemary, and butter. Add on top. Toss to combine.
3. Grill for 12 minutes.
4. Serve and enjoy.

NUTRITION:

Calories: 150
Proteins: 5 g.
Carbs: 7 g.
Fat: 15 g.

200. SMOKED COLESLAW

PREPARATION TIME:
15'

COOKING TIME:
25'

SERVINGS:
8

INGREDIENTS:

1 purple cabbage, shredded
1 green cabbage, shredded
2 scallions, sliced
1 cup carrots, shredded

For the dressing:
1 tbsp. celery seed
1/8 cup white vinegar
1 ½ cups mayo
Black pepper and salt to taste

DIRECTIONS:

1. Preheat the grill to 180ºF with a closed lid.
2. On a tray, spread the carrots and cabbages. Place the tray on the grate and smoke for about 25 minutes.
3. Transfer to the fridge to cool.
4. In the meantime, make the dressing. In a bowl, combine the ingredients. Mix well.
5. Transfer the veggies to a bowl. Drizzle with the sauce and toss
6. Serve sprinkled with scallions.

NUTRITION:
Calories: 35 g.
Protein: 1 g.
Carbs: 5 g.
Fat: 5 g.

CONCLUSION

Wood Pellet Smoker and Grill is made with heavy-duty black powder-coated steel construction and has 2 fireboxes that can accommodate up to 24–40 lbs. bags of wood pellets, 1 for smoking meat and another for making BBQ. With its patented hood system, you can monitor each stage of your cooking, from grilling chicken to smoking bacon with ease. The system is designed to provide you with a consistent temperature that will not fluctuate throughout the cooking process. You can set your desired temperature and monitor the internal meat temperature, so you do not overcook your meat or burn it by setting its automatic timer for a slower cooking process.

When you put a smoker to the proper use and use the most significant kind of pellets, the flavor induced is so distinctive that not only you but also every guest who ends up eating the food is sure to be amazed at the exceptional culinary skills you possess. Most of these recipes allow you to make a little makeshift if you are missing out on some ingredients. However, to get the best results, we want you to stick to the details as closely as possible.

So, make the most of this stunning cookbook and try these recipes so that you could take your food buds for a real ride.

You have to ensure that you end up buying the most remarkable kind of smokers and utilize the perfect pellets, or else you will miss out on getting the real authentic flavor for these ideal recipes. Refine them a little if you so desire, but I believe they are as perfect as you would want them to be.

Here are some of the things we should keep in mind while getting the right barbecue grill:

- Be careful of the size when deciding on the right barbecue grill. We must be mindful of the usage of the grill because it will determine the extent of it. It can so happen one might want to throw a big party where they will need to have a big barbecue handy. On the other hand, someone might want to grill their veggies and proteins on a chilly winter evening on a more compact grill.

- All barbecue grills are not the same. So, the design of the grill will play an essential role in choosing the right grill. One factor to consider is the ease of assembly of the barbecue. Certain grills need no tools to assemble. But we might also encounter barbecues which might require a lot of tools for assembly. It would be prudent to go for barbeques which are easier to assemble.

- Apart from the design of the grill, assess what accessories we get with it. For example, if we want to put our food on the grill, then your grill should have or can accommodate a grill set. Also, we should check whether the hood of the grill has a Smoke Temperature gauge that is readable or not. Lastly, a couple of utensil holders and hooks along with a stainless-steel meat thermometer is a bonus.

- The right barbeque meat is heavily dependent on the kind of grills used. Use this guide and the different recipes in this cookbook to try your hands at other barbeque preparations from around the globe!

So, be all set to enjoy the excellent cooking times.

Manufactured by Amazon.ca
Bolton, ON

42845296R00125